Turning My Pain into Purpose

By

Renee I. Campos

DEDICATION

I dedicate this book to every person reading it, and I want to tell you that after the storm, there is always calm. No matter how strong the storm hits, stand strong like a tree and don't be moved or shaken. We will face many giants in life, but just know that you've got this — this too shall pass. There is nothing too big or too small that you cannot beat in life. Just breathe, smile, dust off your feet, and keep moving. Remember, one step at a time to greatness! Remember, we all have greatness inside of us; we just have to unlock our gifts and passions within.

I dedicate this book to everyone who has supported me on my writing journey. To the women out there who pick up this book, just know: you are queens and warriors! And to the men: you are kings and warriors!

To new beginnings…

ACKNOWLEDGMENTS

I want to thank my heavenly Father up above; this would not be possible if it were not for Him. We are all authors of our own story. What is your story? Whatever it is, never be afraid to share it, whether it's good or bad. Thank you to my publisher and editor once again for allowing me to share my story and continue this journey as a writer. Thank you to all the women who have walked this journey with me, helping, encouraging, and, most of all, empowering me. I also want to thank my three children—Crystal, Christopher, and Estefani—my mother, my siblings Janet, Javier, Barbara, and Efrain, and my family, but most of all, my every single friend who is walking this journey with me.

I also want to thank my ex-husband for walking out and removing himself from my path. We were only meant to be with each other for a short time. I don't live in regrets. But I have learned a lot about myself and have become the strong and powerful woman I am today. I don't thank you; I thank God for taking me through this ugly and tough journey to prepare me for the next. I still thank you and don't hate you, but at this new table that my Father is preparing, only a few will sit with me, and unfortunately, you're not one of them. You were part of my journey for a moment, but our time together has concluded. I will remember very few memories, but I will never resent you. Even though you tried to break me, it only made me stronger!

I am stronger than ever. I have learned from my mistakes, but I don't regret them. These were just lessons for the next chapter of my journey, and here I am, writing my next chapter, but you're not part of it. They only made me strong. I know that writing might not come easy to some, but to those who have the passion and put in the work, don't stop — just keep on writing because it's a gift that our Father has given you. Many will love your book, or others might not even read it, but most of all, it's your book, you created it, it's your life, it's your passion, but most of all, it's your story.

I never really shared much about him because I was in a dark and toxic place for about eight years and away from home. Through this time apart, we had to find ourselves and love ourselves before we could reconnect as a whole. My journey with him in my first book was an ugly one and one that I thought was the end of our toxic relationship. Well, boy, was I wrong. We once again reconnected, but not knowing it would be for a short period before filing for divorce — a not-so-pretty one that I am still battling with. But that will not stop me from striving and fighting till the end. What has tried to break me for so many years will only make me a stronger and more resilient person who I am today. I don't live in regrets because we had to reunite again to realize that this relationship was not healthy but rather ugly and toxic. We were both trying to hang on to it. Well, here I am today, persevering and stronger than ever. Now I can say that I've thrown out the garbage that was getting old in my life. This marriage was an eye-opener experience, but most of all, it helped me to work on myself.

I know that when we find ourselves in toxic relationships, we often blame the other person and look for reasons to leave because there comes a point where the mind and soul get drained. We don't want to continue to fight to stay, so we run. It's so easy to run away from the problem and hard to fight for what you want in a relationship. Some of us want things our way, but this is where you compromise, and always remember to agree and disagree.

Although we are not in a good place but in the place that we both need to be at this moment, this book is not about us but about the journey of self-love and self-care. I faced many challenges, but here I am today, speaking about them and the things I would not repeat. It takes patience always being quick to listen and slow to speak, although it's not easy. A special person that came into my life in my darkest moments, he never gave up on me till this day, I want to say although this journey has been like a rollercoaster, you never got off you stood by my side on this journey even if it was from afar but you never gave up on us, thank you for not judging me, accepting me for me. A new beginning to greatness involves getting rid of negative things, thoughts, and people. There is no room for garbage. A new beginning to greatness involves getting rid of negative things, thoughts, and people. There is no room for garbage; garbage belongs in the dumpster for a reason—it's old, it stinks, and it needs to be thrown out. Just like garbage, if we don't throw it out daily, it begins to stink. The same applies to toxic people in our lives. Throw them out; don't wait until you see gnats. We need to renew our minds and thoughts every day—from our mind, body, and soul.

Table of Contents

CHAPTER 1
WOMAN YOU ARE A QUEEN

When is it time to let go? I said, "How long does a woman have to devalue herself? Love yourself, 'Queen.' It's called self-love. Fall in love with yourself, and you will find fulfillment. You will find yourself falling in love with you, not just with a person. Don't settle for the first person that comes along. First, take your time and fall in love with your mind, body, and soul. Remember, these three things are sacred, and not just anyone deserves them—only one person who loves you, respects you, adores you, values you, and, most of all, respects you. Women know your place and your worth.

Not everyone has someone to mentor them as a child, teen, or even as an adult. We all have our life journey, and we don't have a guide on how we are supposed to live life. We just live one day at a time—some good, some bad, and some ugly. But we know that everything has its beginning and its ending. Our life story begins the moment we are born and ends the day we part from this world. Remember, we are only passing through, but in the meantime, let's ask ourselves how we are going to live it. Not everyone is

1

born rich or in a good home — some are, some aren't. But that doesn't mean we can't overcome and be successful in life. It's not about what we've been through in life; it's where you are going in life. It's not how you start the race but how you finish it.

Let the past stay in the past and the future in the future, but let us live in the moment and in the present. Live it as if it were your last day. Growing up as a young child and teen, I had very low self-esteem. I felt like the black sheep compared to my two sisters. I felt left out a lot because I didn't feel I had my parents to look up to, nor did I have a mentor to guide me. Throughout my teens and young adult years, I always wanted to fit in. I felt insecure about myself and just wanted to be part of something, searching for love in all the wrong places. I hung around the wrong crowd in high school; they weren't the best example. Although I saw things I shouldn't have seen, I knew in my heart of hearts that I wouldn't do what my friends did growing up. I went through a lot of mental and emotional abuse from family members, even though they didn't know they were doing it. But it was normal for them. Mental or emotional abuse doesn't only come from a spouse; it can come from a parent, sibling, friend, boyfriend, girlfriend, co-worker, or even a manager.

Here I am today, speaking to many of you who have walked in my shoes and might still be there. I don't judge you; just don't stay there for too long. Some say life is like a journey, and I believe it is. You never know who will come into your life and when they will leave. There will be roadblocks and challenges on your journey, but what counts is how you face them and overcome them.

CHAPTER 2
TIME HEALS ALL PAIN

A really good friend of mine once said, "The past is history, the present is a gift, and the future is a mystery." This is true. The past is called the past for a reason—it came, and it's gone. It's not meant for you to bring into your future or stay there either. Sometimes, we bring the old into the new, which can be difficult. When one door closes, you might think, "I have a fresh start now," but if you don't close the previous chapter of your past, it will keep intruding into your present. You can't move forward into what the present has for you. When we don't let go of the past, it feels like we are still carrying an anchor on our legs. Believe it or not, we can become slaves to our past hurt, almost like chains that need to be broken. We can be free from what was holding us down. It's an ugly feeling when there is no freedom, and we carry so much weight that we just don't let go, or maybe we just don't know how to let go. Carrying your past is like carrying a heavy weight that keeps getting heavier and heavier.

Today, I look at each day as a new beginning. What happened yesterday, whether good or bad, has come and gone. As I reflect on every day, I think about the good and the bad, the things I can change, and how I can change them. For the things I can't change, I trust and believe in God that He has it under control. I know some might think that people don't change — that was me.

Let me rewind eight years ago. I reconnected with a very good friend of mine. Yes, he was not in a good place, and neither was I — hurt, broken, and just getting out of a bad relationship. But he always encouraged me and never judged me. Unfortunately, he found himself in a place of incarceration and faced the consequences of his bad choices. But who am I to judge? All I wanted to do was be there for him because we grew up together from a very young age. Although you grow up close to someone, it doesn't always mean you know them until you marry them or even live with them. Then, you continue to grow and learn from each other. Fast forward eight years. I thought that this journey of being a new author was going to be one I had to walk alone, but that's not the case. I am so grateful for all the wonderful people I have met along the way. Some were just passing through to help and then left, while others have stayed to walk this journey with me.

These past ten years have been life-changing. From being scared, lonely, depressed, and codependent, I have become an independent, single parent, warrior, and queen. I am now in a place where I embrace all of my imperfections and learn from them. No longer do I live in regrets—I live in victory, learning from everything I had to encounter. I am who I am today because of everything I had to face on this journey. Would I change anything? No, because I believe that everything presented to every human being is for a season and a reason. It's to prepare us for what we are going to be shaped and molded to become. I once heard a woman say, "I'd rather be a rock than a sponge," and you know, I understood the meaning behind that because, in life, you can be a sponge, have a pity party, and be depressed.

CHAPTER 3
BEING A MOM AND DAD

I am a single parent, and life has thrown a lot of challenges my way, but I did not waver. Here I am today, continuing this journey. I just finished my first book in the last week of June. I was amazed to believe it was done and ready to be published. I didn't know where to begin to tell people it was out, but everyone was excited and looking forward to what the future holds for me and the opportunities that will open up. Although 2022 was supposed to be my year, I think it was a year of breakthroughs, releasing hurt, pain, and forgiveness, but most of all, working on myself.

These past six months, and the months to come, have been full of surprises, but most importantly, they have been about becoming a better me — loving myself and embracing the new me. Is it easy? Not at all. I have never been alone, always with a partner or married, but I have been by myself for the past eight-plus years. Although I was married, we were not together, but that story is told in my first book if you read it.

Today is all about finding true love in yourself. How do you start? By being good to yourself, resting, feeding your body good things, telling yourself affirmations, and always smiling in the mirror as you get ready. Some people think it's crazy to talk to yourself — they might think you're crazy or losing your marbles — but no, it's called loving yourself. Try it. I think you will love it and do it every day. Waking up is a gift; no one promises to wake up every day, but we go to sleep and believe that we will wake up, right? It's called faith. Take care of the internal, but also the external, and most of all, the emotional.

CHAPTER 4
BREAKING TIDES

Why do we have to break tides? Some of us start with a gang of people and think every single one might have our backs, but your circle begins to get smaller and smaller when you are in the darkest moments of your life. When you call the people you trust, they are nowhere to be found, even your own family. Your family can be a small or large group — it doesn't matter. It's the loyalty and the moments that they are there for you in the good, the bad, and the ugly that count. Unfortunately, that is not the case for some of us.

I am not here to judge anyone or to tell anyone to cut people out of their lives — that is something you have to learn how to deal with. Whether it's family or someone you're with, you should never stay in a relationship just because you don't want to hurt the other person's feelings or because you made a vow. Love is not supposed to hurt, be abusive, or demean. I know that not every challenging marriage or situation has a good ending. Every day is a fight because the war is real, as we battle with so much from the moment we open our eyes. I believe that when you allow the enemy an inch, he will take a yard. If you rely solely on your own understanding, things will also go wrong.

My favorite scripture, which I first learned in the Bible, is from the book of Proverbs 3:5-6: "Trust in the Lord with all your heart, and do not lean on your own understanding; in all your ways acknowledge Him, and He shall direct your path." Well, we made a wrong turn and fell out of God's plan, but now we are getting back on God's path.

CHAPTER 5
HOW CAN YOU FORGIVE IF YOU HAVEN'T FORGIVEN YOURSELF?

If you think for a moment, you can recall many mistakes you've made in life and how many people forgave you. But how many times have you forgiven others or even yourself? I am my own worst critic, and I have been hard on myself when I've made bad choices. It takes me a very long time to forgive myself. This was something I didn't know how to change, so I had to learn through life experience. But I would never want anyone to go through what I went through. Always know that it is okay to make mistakes. Don't regret them; just learn from them and move on. However, don't keep making the same mistakes because if you do, they will grow into bigger problems that will eventually hurt you and the people around you. Love yourself, empower yourself, but most of all, value yourself. Never, never settle. Always dream big, even for the impossible, because nothing is impossible. We can achieve and strive for anything that we put our minds to. But remember, nothing in life is easy; you have to work hard to earn it, and there are no shortcuts.

Don't let one bad person spoil what God has planned for your life. Some people are like the seasons—some come and go, while others are here to stay for a lifetime. Sometimes, it's okay to be alone; it's better to be safe than sorry. At least you know that God's gift is greater than the gift of the world. God will only bring good things when we wait on Him. When we go ahead of God's will, we don't know what lies ahead. Sometimes, there can be so much destruction, pain, or suffering. The Lord will help us through that turmoil, but He will always give us red flags so that we don't take the wrong path. You see, the Lord is like a road map; without Him, we are lost. Maybe some believe, or perhaps they don't, but we have to ask ourselves what road map is guiding our lives—are we winning or losing? There are people who can be happy and even successful in life, but when no one is around in that dark place, we all have moments when we are alone. But are we happy regardless of whether we have money or not? I'd rather be ten times happier and full of joy than have all the money in the world and live miserably. Not even all the money in the world will stop a person from dying or from a fatal disease. You see, money is temporary, just like our life. We are just passing through on Earth; we are not eternal on Earth, but we are eternal with our Heavenly Father. So, the next time you say you want to be rich, think again—this will only be for a season and not eternal. We should desire to be good in the time we have on Earth, for our family, community, and our jobs. Let us not look at our job as just a paycheck but as an opportunity to be great and to help those around us. We don't know what battles they are fighting in their lives. I'd rather see someone happy and not suffering than someone flashing money or showing off how much they have.

A pastor once said, be careful who you allow into your life because you don't know what kind of demons you are inviting in. It sounds crazy, but when you think about it, it's true. For one, a lot of people don't really know the person or where they are coming from, and it can take a while to get to know someone. Some of us don't give the relationship time to develop, to get to know each other very well, and to understand their intentions. I have come to understand how bad codependency can become and how it can affect a person. I found myself, all my life, always needing to please someone, wanting to be validated, or being in a relationship—never knowing what it meant to be alone, just to be free and love yourself. I am getting to that place of freedom, and yes, it can be a good feeling, but it is also scary because if you don't occupy your mind, you become lonely and start to feel like you have to be with someone. Sometimes, it's okay to be by yourself. Some of us have been so hurt so many times that we get used to it, and it becomes normal. Then, you attract what you allow into your life, and not everything that walks into your path is good for you.

We must learn from our bad choices in life, but we must never live in regrets or blame ourselves. They are not regrets; they are life lessons that will teach us to become greater and stronger. I know I have made a lot of bad choices in life and good ones, too, but I could have avoided a lot of heartache.

CHAPTER 6
DON'T LIVE IN REGRETS;
THOSE ARE JUST LESSONS

We will soon meet again, we do not say goodbye but see you later.

I spent all my life living in regret and beating myself up for years, calling myself an idiot and stupid. "How could you do that? Why? Look at you now." But one day, I said to myself, "No more will I condemn myself and be the victim. I will get up, dust my feet off, straighten my crown, and keep moving." My scars in life are a reminder of where I've been, but they have allowed me to be here today, to speak about it, learn from it, and empower those who have gone through or are going through something and feel stuck. I said to myself for several years, "I am tired of feeling stuck." I always remember: if I don't like something, then change it. Do something about it and stop complaining because this is not going to get me anywhere.

Growing up, you're not given a book of life on how every stage of your life is going to be. Some of us had both mother and father, and some didn't, or maybe just one parent. Some might have lived in a group home, with a family member, or even been adopted. I felt like I grew up alone with my siblings because my mom worked hard to ensure we had clothes and food on the table. Growing up, I wanted to be loved—not necessarily by a man, but just to have a role model in my life. I didn't have that, so as I got older and began to date, codependency began. Even before that, I started getting closer to two of my uncles and experienced things that a young pre-teen shouldn't have. If you read my first book, "My Scars Tell My Story," you would understand what I am referring to. As a teen, I started dating at the age of 12. What does a 12-year-old girl know about dating? Well, I thought I knew something. The one thing I knew I wanted was attention and love from someone, and it felt good. But

I was so young—what did I really know about love? Every three months, I felt like I had a new boyfriend. I would get bored and just tell them, "I don't want to be with you anymore." I was not sexually active, thank God. I was still a virgin and never gave myself to any man but the one I was going to marry. I waited, although I am no longer married to him. I was married to him for 18 years, and he gave me three beautiful children.

I can't really remember being happy, except for a picture I saw one day when I was turning 5 years old. My grin was ear to ear; I was so pleased. Sometimes, I think about the scripture in Matthew 18:3, where Jesus says we need to have childlike faith—trusting and believing without worrying. That's how I interpret that picture. I know that the Bible also says not to be anxious about anything but to pray and supplicate. I have to always minister to myself when I am going through a storm. I wasn't always very outspoken and vocal. I never knew how to speak up for myself. I was very shy growing up, very naive and believed everything people would tell me—even people I dated. I feel I was very gullible and too kind-hearted, with a big heart that people would take for granted. But I am grateful that those people just came into my life and are now gone. They served their purpose in my life, whether for good or bad. I know I would not be in the place I am today if I hadn't gone through what I did.

Fast forward to now, in my forties. The reason I speak of this time is because of where we are living today. I know that what I write about now in the present is what I am going through right now as I write. It is so real, and I am living it. It's fresh in my mind, and I can pour my all into this book.

This is not the only reason why I felt so broken — not just because of the bad relationships I went through, but also just from growing up. I was not in a good environment and was not protected by the people who were supposed to love me or even by adults in general. All my life, I blamed myself for my bad choices. I had to learn everything the hard way and on my own. I had to make my own choices, whether good or bad, and they both had their consequences. Growing up, I felt there was always someone trying to break me, but they never succeeded. Even to this day, I never understood why people hate or envy others. I have always felt that way on many different occasions, but when I pour my heart out to them, they take a step back and rethink how they perceive me, even though they don't know me. It's okay because even the Bible says, "You will know them by their fruits." It's all about action because actions speak louder than words. Well, as the saying goes, you kill them with kindness.

Not everyone in life is going to like you, even if you haven't done anything wrong, and that is okay because your energy and your presence will speak for itself. All my life, I always lived to please people. Yes, it's true and sad. But even though it took me this long, it's okay because I get it now — stop trying to please people and know your worth. If people can't respect or value you, then walk with your head up high and with a purpose.

As I go through this second writing journey in my life, not only have I fallen in love with writing, but I think of everything I can be grateful for. Just to have faith and believe that when I close my eyes, I will wake up tomorrow — yes, that is faith. When I awake, I am thankful for another day — to walk, talk, eat, have a roof over my head, food on the table, to give, forgive, and most of all, to love. Not everything that comes or happens in our life is going to make us happy, like the people that will cross our path. I never knew how good self-care and self-love could bring so much love and peace into your life. How can people not want to try it? Well, I can say some might say, "I don't have time in my busy schedule." I have learned that even five minutes goes a long way. The moment you open your eyes, it's a moment of gratefulness. Another day of life. Yesterday came and went; we can't go back and fix yesterday's mistakes, but we can learn from them and create new beginnings today. I am so grateful for the desire I have to love and give back. I know I don't have much, but the little that I have, I want to give to anyone that crosses my path.

Working in the medical field opens up so many desires—not only to study more about healthcare but also to go into that field. Currently, I am working on my Bachelor's Degree in Social Work for families. I believe that we should never forget where we come from. Everyone's journey is uniquely made, so we all have different paths in life. Some have it harder than others, but no matter your battle, we all have to fight our own. It doesn't matter how hard it may get; that's when we have to be the strongest. It will get worse before it gets better, but you will come out strong. As we walk through this journey called life, we can all face it with a positive attitude, complain about the circumstances of life, or face it and fight through it. I will never say that life is easy because it's not. Some of our journeys have been full of turmoil and losses, but at the same time, I promise it will build you up to be a stronger person than when you started.

Every morning, as we rise to another day, we should never forget that we made it to another day. Yesterday is gone, and today is a new day. Yesterday's troubles were yesterday's, and we are given a new day to start fresh. As we look in the mirror, we can tell ourselves, "We got this. This, too, shall pass. You are great, you are awesome, you are beautiful, you are a warrior, you're not a quitter, but most of all, you are a queen." As I write this book, I continue to speak affirmations to myself. Sometimes, when no one is around, only you, you only—you can do two things: isolate yourself or speak powerful words into your existence.

All my life, I was surrounded by negative words, like, "If you don't go to school, that is your problem. You will not achieve what you want. You will become pregnant and not graduate." "You will get pregnant and drop out of school." Well, guess what? I graduated from high school, got married, and had three beautiful children. Then, I went back to school to get my degree in Social Work. So, I am not sure who they were speaking to because I did the opposite of what people said I would do. Never let anyone dictate your future or let your past define your present because it cannot define who you want to become and will be. I know for some, it's hard—maybe you were bullied and have low self-esteem. Even though I didn't get bullied, I did have very, very low self-esteem all my life.

I always worried about what people thought of me, and I was a people pleaser. Don't ever worry about what others think of you or do things just to please another person—you will never be happy. Why wait until you are damaged by something or someone? Work on you and start now. Today, we can set a goal or date to start taking care of ourselves. How can we take care of others when we can't even take care of ourselves? Even the bible tells us that our bodies are a temple, and we must not mistreat it. I never knew what self-care or self-love was. All I knew was that I wanted to give love and get it back in return, but that was never the case. As women and men, we don't have to get personal validation to feel we are worth something. We are enough. No matter what in life, someone has told you that you were worthless or always demeaned you or put you down, you are powerful, you are strong, you can do anything that you set your mind to, and never be afraid to take risks in life, of course, there are good risks and bad ones but the good ones it takes having faith and just trusting your instinct.

Depression, who can speak on this many for sure I know that a lot of us have suffered from some kind of depression. Statistics from The National Institute of Mental Health (NIMH) estimate that 16.2 million U.S. adults had at least one major episode of severe depression in 2016. This represents 6.7 percent. Depression is most common in ages 18 - 25. A story of my life of depression, I will take you back to the first time I experienced it. I didn't even know I had it. Just so you know, not all depression is bad. The reason why I say this is because there are different types of depression. The ones that come to mind are postpartum depression, the loss of a family member, or a tragic change of event. The question here is, how do you handle depression? Well, when I first experienced it, it was when I had my first child.

I don't know. One day, I was sitting at the table eating with my ex-husband and mother-in-law, and out of nowhere, I started crying for no reason. I just got up and went to my room and continued to cry, not knowing why. One Sunday at church, I shared it with a member of the church, and she told me that it was called postpartum depression. I wish someone had warned me, not even the doctors told me. You see, depression comes in many forms and at different times of our lives. Some can be only sadness or something that you could be going through, but when it prolongs, and you just don't have any reason to live, then that's where the problem is and you have to talk to someone.

I fell into a deep depression when my husband kept traveling and never at home. We argued so much, and I was getting tired of living this way. As our relationship got worse then, it became abusive, and he also was unfaithful. Our marriage just went downhill. I felt like I didn't want to live anymore. I had nowhere or anyone to turn to because everyone thought we were the perfect couple. Don't ever wait until it gets worse and think it's going to get better. Love is not supposed to hurt. Love is kind. Love is not sadness nor abuse. Never be afraid to speak out if you can't at that moment, but do it before it gets worse. Yes, they always say that it will get worse before it gets better.

Family is everything to us, but are they there when you really need them? Well, you have to always remember that we all walk through our different journeys in life. For some, we are alone, and others are very close to family members and cherish them. I love my siblings, but we all grew apart as we all became adults. Division happens. The only time we gather together is when someone passes away, and that's sad that it has to take that to happen to see everyone. Don't ever take anyone for granted, regardless of your difference. One day, you're here. The next moment, you are gone. You see, on earth, we have a relationship with each other, and we never imagine that we will lose a loved one, but that day will come. I just know that no one is ever prepared, but one thing I can say is that we need to begin to live, live life to the fullest and live like today is our last day. Trials will come, and storms will come, but just hang on because after the storm there is always a calm. There is always a reason why we face challenges in life, to grow to get to where we need to go. Who said life is easy? No one says it only gets harder, but we get stronger.

Don't let the problem control you, but you can control it, yes it is easier said than done, but let me put it this way, In challenges you encounter, you might not have the solution to the problem, but you do have the solution on how you deal with the problem, Everything has a solution.   Throughout life, I always reacted to my fears and insecurity, like the same goes you fight or flight. Yes, that was me for so many years. Your body naturally reacts to trouble internally or externally. It's how you react when your brain feels danger approaching that you will see the end results of that reaction. I had to stop, think, breathe, and respond. I can think of so many reasons to get stressed and walk around feeling sorry for myself, but I choose not to. From growing up with a single parent to getting molested at a young age, finding myself in more than one abusive relationship as a young adult, and then losing my kids' father to a severe motorcycle accident that now left him wheelchair-bound. Losing my brother at 38, I can tell you the horrific stories that I have endured so much; but I don't want to focus on the losses but on the victories in my life. My ex is dead but alive in a wheelchair and a whole other person.

The Bible says that the wage of sins is death, but for some, he spares, and some are not here today, and that will be something that we will never understand today. I look at life, or I want to look at life as if it was my last day here on earth, yes it might sound depressing, but no, I am just telling myself self that I want to live each day as happy and grateful as I can be because no one is promised today or tomorrow. I want to leave this earth knowing that I made someone happy or many and that I pour love into those who need a glimpse of it each day. I want to impact people's lives and have so much to be thankful for that god has done in my life today. I should not be here today.

I didn't have a happy childhood. Had no father, and my mother always worked, had no guidance, and had very low self-esteem. Got married at eighteen, had my three children at a young age, and began to experience abuse in my marriage for many years until one day, be confronted with something so tragic happening in my life and felt like my whole had just caved in on me and not knowing how to raise my children by myself, and even paying my own bills.

Ladies, never, never rely on anyone to guide you unless it's for empowerment and greatness but always walk with your head high and never low because you are not weak. Throughout life or even when we are little, yes, we look up to our parents or to adults. Still, there comes a point in our lives that we have to let go and fly on our own. We must do that, and why? Because if we don't, we can find ourselves crippled and not know how to walk on our own and make our own choices. It's sad how, in today's world, we see how there are women who are controlled by men or just even codependent on men. For some, we might say we trust our husbands. He is the head; yes, this is true, but you are not under his feet. You are supposed to walk beside him. Every woman should feel like a queen, valued and respected. When was the last time your boyfriend, partner, or husband opened the door for you? Not only is this a gentleman, but he honors you, respects you, and values you. He wants to always allow you before him and let the world know this is my queen. You are opening up the door for your queen. To some, it might sound old fashioned, or call it what you want, but any woman, I guarantee they will feel like a queen and a person doesn't have to do all these things but a honeymoon should never be over after a year or two after getting married, the honeymoon should be every day for the rest of the time we are here on earth. Well, this book is not just focused on marriage or couples, but it's focused on you, your body, mind, and soul at the end of the day. Love you, and you first.

CHAPTER 7
WHEN WAS THE LAST TIME YOU LOVED YOURSELF

How can you say you love someone if you can't love yourself? I know many women give so much and forget to love themselves because all we want is to give, and we forget that our bodies and minds also need attention. I have learned in this past year of the pandemic how important it is to take care of yourself, especially in the times we are living in. We need to, even more so, never take our health for granted. Meditate, sleep, eat, and exercise, even if you never have before. It's never too late to start. I had to change my lifestyle and believe me, it has been the hardest thing I've had to do. Some start slow, and some can't change overnight, but no matter where you start, just start somewhere. It all begins with rest. Take care of your body and mind. Don't fill them with toxic conversations or toxic foods; they just lead to toxicity and garbage in our souls. Self-love, self-care, empower yourself every morning and start by saying something positive to bring out good, positive energy for your day. Today is going to be a good day. Today, I will speak positively, even when there is negative energy. I will overcome evil with good. I will speak positive words to someone today. Speak affirmations into your soul every day. Speak positivity into your existence. This is the power of the Law of Attraction. Speak it into your existence. "OMG" works. We are closing this year of 2024 and entering into a great and powerful beginning of an awesome and amazing year. I will enter the New Year with my second book. I am so blessed to finally start editing this second book and many more to come if you want to follow my story and read my first book. My Scars tell my story and walk on this journey with me. Together, we have the power to change, not just for me but for every woman who picks up this book. Remember, don't read it as just a book but as a tool to empower yourself and become the greater, awesome "queen" that you are meant to be. If you can take away something from this book, let it change you as it has for me and many other women who have read my first book. Now, walk with me in every book that the Lord will allow me to write.

Every day is a new day, and it comes and goes. Whatever happened on that specific day, we cannot change the good or bad, but we can learn, move on, and strive to be greater than we were yesterday. Set a goal for yourself, not just because the New Year is close, but to look back and see how far you have come. At the end of every year, I sit down and look at my vision board and calendar for the New Year, and I write down what I want to accomplish for that year. I start with three-month, six-month, and one-year goals.

For long-term goals, I have a one-year, three-year, and five-year plan. This book is not to organize your life but to share what has worked and continues to work for me. It keeps me motivated because I look forward to what is to come. I am more of a visual person, so I know that if I see something, I look forward to it. Versus just having it in my thoughts, which means there's a 99 percent chance I probably won't do it. I won't sit here and tell you that I am the most organized person because I would be lying to you, but I try to maintain some type of stability and organizational skills.

Remember, at the beginning of my book, I was very codependent. I always had someone to guide me and hold my hand in decision-making. This was a big mistake. When you allow this, it makes you handicapped, and you are not able to be successful because it will take you longer to accomplish something or not accomplish it at all. I say this because, believe it or not, I got my driver's license at the age of 40. This is what I mean by allowing a person or people to tell you they will do it for you or even control what you do and when you do it. Absolutely not. That's not you. You need to stop. You've got this. You are awesome, you are stronger, you are a warrior, amazing, and great. You can do anything you put your mind to.

CHAPTER 8
BEING UNCOMFORTABLE IS A GOOD THING

Being uncomfortable is a good thing because it is a sign that you are getting out of your comfort zone. I was not always as outspoken as I am today. Never in a million years would you have caught me speaking in front of a crowd, let alone writing a book. What happens in life happens, and I said to myself only two things can happen: I can crawl into a hole and have a pity party, or I can do something about it. I chose to change. Change is hard—who said it was easy? I am a very stable person, and when my life requires change, it's hard, but if it's to grow, I have to get out of my comfort zone and keep climbing up the ladder. I don't want to be left behind.

What motivated me to write my first book? It took me being bed-bound after surgery—I couldn't walk or move for eight weeks. I can't remember how many Netflix shows I watched. I knew I had to do more than just rest and watch shows, so I began looking up publishers. Finally, I got a call from one, and they were interested in hearing my story. At first, I thought it was a scam, but the calls kept coming. When I spoke to the publisher, I couldn't believe they were interested in my book. So, I picked up my writing where I had left off. Even though I was procrastinating, he really motivated me to finish it. He kept telling me, "You only have a little to go. You got this, and I know you can do it."

I was empowered, and when I finished my first book, and now I am about to publish my second book, I would have never imagined I would be publishing a book, let alone a second one; this has only motivated me to continue writing. I want to keep writing until I can't write anymore. I can now see myself writing as a career—it is the best thing I have ever done. I am so grateful for the passion and desire that continues to grow. I want to speak more about the Law of Attraction.

I will continue to write as long as I am able to. Writing has been my therapy journey for the past eight years. I have been through a rollercoaster that I feel I can't get off, but I know that my day is coming to get off it and embark on my beautiful journey of joy, growth, and prosperity, which I have been waiting for a long time. 2024 hasn't been the best year, but I do see the light at the end of the tunnel. I just need to remove some roadblocks from my path to keep moving. Confusion is my worst enemy these days. As soon as things seem to be going okay, other obstacles arise. I ask myself if it is a sign I need to caution myself or if it's just trying to stop me from what awaits me. Well, I know that six to ten months from now, I will be in a better place in every aspect.

Never rush, love. People tend to think that you need to find someone at a certain time in their life or have a child at a certain age—not true. Love yourself first before anyone else. Once you have reached that, love and respect will be given to you. If you love yourself, but all you do is give, give, and give, guess what? You will be disappointed because all you will be doing is giving and not receiving. Yes, this was me for many years, even until today. I stand here today speaking about it because there is nothing wrong with being a very giving person. It just means that you have a great and amazing heart. It's the people we give it to who don't know how to cherish it. They will take you for granted and hurt you, but when they realize that they've hurt you, it's too late to fix it because it could be very broken. A broken heart is not so easy to mend.

CHAPTER 9
THE WAY YOU START YOUR DAY IS THE WAY YOUR DAY WILL TURN OUT

I didn't really believe this at first, but it's so true: the moment you wake up, the thoughts that run through your mind will determine how your day will be. This is why, when you get up, even though many may be tired, you don't have to stay in that state, right? Correct. Once you begin to speak affirmations to yourself—like "today is going to be a great day, and I will have a great and productive day"—every positive word you say plays a big part in shaping your day or week. I'm not going to say that nothing bad will happen throughout your day or week because things can, but how you receive and react to them will impact your mood. You can choose to be angry because someone is rude, or you can say, "Maybe that person is having a bad day, and it's not about me." It's our attitude that determines the outcome.

Sometimes, I don't know how I've made it this far when I think about everything I've gone through and where I am today. I am forever grateful. Is it easy? No, it's still hard. Being a single parent of three children, the sole provider, a book writer, the CEO/Founder of a foundation, attending school part-time, and working full-time—hmmm, I don't know what to say. It's God's grace, mercy, and strength.

Why is it so hard to let go? I never understood why I always felt bad when I had to cut ties with someone. I was a people pleaser, and although I sometimes still find myself that way, it's not as much as before. I have always thought about others before myself, but that didn't always give me positive results. We're in 2024, and the journey continues. Why is it that when we are leaving an old year to enter a New Year, we look forward to the New Year? I know I'm not the only one who feels this way; many can relate to what I'm saying. I started with so much focus and determination, but what has been hard for me in this New Year is letting go of the past and the hurt. Yes, we want to complain, play the victim, and be validated, and even if your friends and family agree or validate your pain, did you gain anything from it? Did we get something out of it, other than resentment, sorrow, and pain, while the other person is moving on with their life?

CHAPTER 10
WHY IS IT SO HARD TO LET GO

This is what I tell myself every day, why am I allowing one person to control my past, present, and future. Suppose I were to write down on a piece of paper the pros and cons we all have to do that. In that case, this doesn't have to be a boyfriend, partner, or friend. It can be anyone that you want to catch tides with. You just don't know how because you don't want to hurt them, or they just won't leave, so you might say ok, so what is the answer to this? Well, some people will just leave even without you leaving them. Some others just won't leave because they think the problem is you they will never admit they are wrong. I believe that you have to follow your heart and always have a good support system that you can trust. Believe me, doing things on your own it's the hardest thing you can do, something you can find yourself. Decisions are always hard, especially if they will impact your present or future, so my advice is to take care of yourself first, rest and self-care and self-love, meditate, and ask god for wisdom to make wise decisions. At the end of the day, no one controls you. Love is not supposed to hurt, love is kind, it is gentle, and not controlling. No matter how life or just your day is, don't quit if you feel you can take another day, rest if you must, but don't quit if you want to cry or scream. Let it all out, but don't quit. Take walks, run, dance, do yoga, or just go to the gym, but don't quit because you know why because this too shall pass.

CHAPTER 11
YOUR DAILY AFFIRMATIONS

What is an affirmation? This is what I asked myself one day, and as I was going through my social media, I saw a motivational women speaker say always speak affirmation over your life daily. You can do them in many ways, speaking to yourself while you are staring at the mirror, putting sticky's on your vision board, or just listening to your favorite motivational speaker. Always remember to change the way you think, and it will change your life. Close your eyes and practice deep breathing. Think of a place, a peaceful place that you once were or even when you were little, the last time you were happy, with no fears, no worries, just peace and joy. Breath deeply and release and tell yourself you got this. This, too, will pass. Not every day is going to be a stress-free day, but I can say that every day is a new start.

A day of stress is how I describe mine. In these past few months, I feel like I don't know where the months have gone. I feel like time is just passing me by, and I am trying to hold on and stop time so I can gather my thoughts, organize my personal life, and have some kind of time management, but between my home, work, and school, I feel like an Octopus but don't have enough arms to juggle my everyday life challenges. All I can do is rest, breathe, and know that at the end of the day, the day has ended, and a new one will soon begin. Yesterday's battles are for yesterday, and today is for today. A real good friend said to me one step at a time, but my head is saying a million steps at a time. I want to do everything but don't have enough time in the day. I am learning to live every day for today and not worry about tomorrow. Sometimes I wonder how life would be if we lived in a perfect world with no sorrow, no pain, no hate, just love and peace, but I guess life was not meant to be perfect because then maybe life would be boring and we wouldn't strive to become greater and strive for what we want in life. I guess there are no shortcuts to reach success, and nothing is handed to us, we all had to work for something at some point in our life. I am glad that we learn from the good, bad, and ugly moments because we learn from them and keep moving. We can't get stuck on what happened yesterday, but we look forward to what tomorrow has for us.

CHAPTER 12
WHY AM I STILL STUCK ON THE PAST

Do you ever find yourself, although you left something or someone in the past, it still seems to be in your present? Can we say why? Well, I can. It's because although we can say that we let go, we honestly never did. Some can let go right away, and for others, it can take months or even years, but for those that can let go, you know there is peace, new doors are open, new people come into our life, and we are not stuck nor our thinking. On the other hand, if we find ourselves still thinking of the past after months or even years, then we will never move to our full potential in life. They will only do the minimal in life and be contemptuous or even unhappy, and what they are holding on to or who they have moved on with their life, and here they are hanging onto the past. It's like having roses trying to grow around a bad weed; if you don't cut the weed, it will just poison the flowers that want to shine and bloom but can't because the old weed is rooted at the bottom of your inner being because you have to hang on to it for so long that it's stuck like a leach. How do you stop holding on to the past, though you would never ask? I had to repeatedly ask myself why am I holding on, did I have guilt, do I care, or did I think I could fix him or this relationship. This is what I tell myself and those who feel the pain, it's ok to hurt, it's ok to cry to be sad, go through the motions but let it go, and don't stay there because what you are doing is giving that person power and they have moved on and you are still stuck. They are not worth your tears anymore. The funeral is over. They are gone from your life. Dust off your shoes, wipe your tears and keep on moving. Keep on elevating and becoming a better you, learn from your mistakes, and know your worth, "Girl." I asked myself all these questions. I was staying with him out of fear, not wanting to stay alone. It was no longer love. For the first time, I can say I have peace, I love myself, and I am no longer afraid to be by myself. I have peace. I have freedom in me. Never feel sorry for yourself. Never settle for a pretty face and pretty talk. If a narcissistic man sees you as weak, then he knows he has you and will sweep you off your feet with charm, which is exactly what happened to me today, not just once but more than once. I would not be speaking on this if I didn't walk in these shoes, but because I have, I want to share what it's like to be fooled, charmed, and even fall deeply in love with a fool who doesn't deserve your heart. Every man should earn his place in a woman's life, and it goes both ways for the men, too. If you meet someone for the first time, you can have an instant connection, but that doesn't mean that you have to trust them on the spot. It's soooo easy to fall for a person because of their status and their personality, but do you know his inner demons, the skeletons he is hiding in the closets. You may ask how we can find all this. Well, you see, there is more time than life. What's the rush to love? Let it be organic. If it is meant to be, it will stay; if it leaves and never comes back, then it was never meant to be. The number one person you should love is yourself, self-care, your inner beauty, then the outside. I always believe in yourself and your capabilities. No one can dictate how you should live your life.

This dark journey doesn't stop; 2024 is supposed to be my year; why is there always something that has to come up. I did my yearly checkup that all us women have to go through, and my test came back with a possible chance of Cancer. I ask myself if god is pushing me for all the bad choices I committed in life. Even though I have been practicing mindful thinking, the thoughts that come and go off the negative possibilities, I say to myself, not today. This is my life, and I will speak life into my life. God gives life, and he will say when it's time to go. I have to walk in victory, not in defeat. I have been to many years that I have been beaten down for far too many years, but the fight is not over until I say it is over. We are all fighters. We all have a warrior in us. Some of us need to wake up that inner warrior in us so we can see and be the warriors we are created to be. Your journey is just beginning so much awaits you. If you are in a good place or where you need to be good for yourself but never be contemptuous, always strive for more always be hungry. You could never have enough in life. If we are in a place where there is no more for us, then give, give back, because remember, once, there was a person who gave to you or invested in you, whether a person, teacher, or mentor, but they gave and because someone gave to you or believed in you, that is why you are where you are. I know that in other stories we have families or people in our life that don't have it well or maybe always had it bad. We all have choices in life. We are given a choice to choose good or evil. This time, I will win the fight, and I will win from beginning to end. If this news had come to me last year or the year before, I think I would be on medication for depression or maybe not even here today, but the person that I have become and continue to change every second of the day is not the person who I am today, I am constantly evolving into the woman that God has created me to be. Can I say if I thought this way a couple of years back? No, not at all. I was hurt, defeated, disappointed, and felt I had no life, I couldn't do this by myself, and I was depressed. Who I have become today is not the same person from yesterday. Every day is a new day, a new chapter, and a new beginning. Whatever happened yesterday has come and gone. Don't be stuck on yesterday, but remember tomorrow will be greater. Some things are out of our control, but what we can control is the way we see and deal with things that we can control. Don't be afraid to love yourself. You don't need a man or anyone to show you love. Love who you are inside out, and then love will find you. You don't even have to look for it. You are created for a purpose; remember that you are not an accident. You were born for something great; everything in life, every battle you face in life, is just another test to prepare you for greatness in life. Never, ever give up on your dream, no matter what anybody does or says to you.

CHAPTER 13
CUTTING OUT PEOPLE THAT DON'T BELONG IN YOUR LIFE

In life, we grow up meeting so many people, but in the future, we can find ourselves either having a bigger circle of friends or even a smaller circle. Why is that? Can you ask yourself do you want to know so many people that they never really look out for your best interest and only look for you when they need something or when you have something they want, or would you rather have a smaller circle of friends, that are your ride or die family and will ride this journey with you through the good and the bad. Well, if you ask me, I have always had a small circle of friends because I have been lied to and betrayed even by the closest people you love and trust. Sometimes, you can't always cut people that are blood. They are your family, but that doesn't mean they have to be part of your circle. They are just family. The ones you can completely cut, cut them and don't turn back. You can give people chances in life once, twice, and even a third time, but when you find giving people even six or seven chances in life, then you are extra nice, and the dumb one is you, not them, because now they are playing you and they know they have you because they know that they can continue to fool you and you will take them back or continue to speak to them. This is called having boundaries for yourself as a person. You have to have a limit, and it's called Enough is enough. Let it be and let it go. Letting go is not an easy thing to do, and I know firsthand experience, but believe me it will bring you so much peace and freedom.

CHAPTER 14
WHEN DO YOU BREAK NEGATIVE PATTERNS

What are negative patterns? Do we even know? I guess I don't. I think I am still trying to figure that out, but I will one day, and when I do, I will be in another place, a place where I can speak and say I've been in a bad and good place, but it's ok if I am there right now because this is why I am writing this book to help myself, and others find their way out of those bad patterns that only hurt us and all we are doing is going in circles and never going anywhere and we just end up at the same place with the same person or in the same situation. Love, what is love? I know that love is an action word, but some people use it lightly or just to make people feel good, but in reality, they hurt those that they should be loving. Some make them feel they love them by hurting them.

This is why we must stop and ask ourselves where we are on this journey. Yes, this is a journey of healing, not just mine but yours. Let us all go for the ride and enjoy it while we heal. Let's start by making a list, a list of the things we love about ourselves and a list of the things we dislike. When we do this, we can start by getting up extra early every morning and begin to meditate the way we want. We can start with 10 minutes, then increase until we find ourselves doing it for 30 minutes. Keep a journal, I know some of us might have people we speak to, and there are those who don't, and we don't know how to get everything out of our chest. Well, guess what? Now you can, and no one can't judge you or tell you you're wrong or tell you you can't speak or shut your mouth. You are free to be you, free to express everything in your heart, good or bad. Treat yourself, yes, go pamper yourself, even if it's once a month, once every 6 months, or even yearly, but remember, do you? I was always told, and still hear it, how can you take care of others if you can't even take care of yourself. Spend alone time, reading, going to the gym, or even spending time with a friend, but do you. We only have one life on this earth. We need to handle it with care inside out. If people in your life don't value you, then cut them out. If they hurt you, cut them out; if they take more, then cut them out. Life is too short to waste time and energy on people that are not worth your time.

I always look forward to the new year, and then it comes, and then when I least expect it, the year has ended, and I tell myself what I accomplished. This is what I am telling you today, we are half into 2024, and what have we seen or what have we done this year? Was it something we wanted to do or we had no choice. For me, I feel like I came into this year hoping for positive results, but I am still waiting. Is that a good or bad thing? Well, I had to tell myself to stop carrying the previous year into the new one if you couldn't accomplish what you wanted this year; there is always next year. Just walk out of this year proud. Well, it came and gone, and you can't go into a new year with an old year still dragging onto you because those things will hold you from seeing the new things that need to happen. It's like this. When you drink a cup of coffee every morning, you want a fresh, hot cup. You don't want leftover cold coffee in your fresh hot coffee because it won't taste good, right. Your fresh start needs a fresh you, not a warn out you but a fresh you. Even if you left unfinished things behind, let it be, let it go because if it never got done or resolved, it was never meant to be. I saw a movie today it was called Bucket List and it was the best movie ever, you know why? It was about two grown people who were dying and only had 6 months to live. In those 6 months, they could sit around their family and have pitting for themselves, or they can live the best 6 months of their life. I am not saying that you should wait until you are lying on your deathbed but saying that we need to live our life every day like it was our last day because once that day is gone, we can't go back because that day came and now its gone, so whatever we did good or bad we can't change it. I know that if we can go back in time and change things in our life and make it better, so many of us would do that I know I would. One thing

I can say is never, never regret your past. Just look at it as lessons learned. I know for some, they might not be lessons but trauma, and those things only time will heal, and for those that feel that they will never heal, you are wrong because you will. We are stronger than we think. We are strong, we are warriors, we are fighters. Yes, we feel, we make mistakes, and we fall, but if we fall, we get back up and dust our feet and continue to walk because that was a bump in our road.

The moments of sadness, and we just don't want to move or do anything. It's ok to feel like you are sad, or you want to cry your heart out, or you're frustrated with your life. Feel the emotions, go through the emotions, and then let it go and keep on moving. You are a human being who has emotions, and you will get tired, and it's your mind and body telling you to stop and rest. If I had a bucket list I would do so many things. First, I would take my kids on a family vacation anywhere they wanted to go, then I would start my journey and travel the world, and along the way, I would give back to those who don't have. If I had all the money in the world or at least live comfortably, I want to give back. I also would create shelters for families and women who have been mistreated and train women to be leaders for other women in the states and other parts of the world. You see, just because you don't have money, it's ok as long as you dream big and the desire is there everything else will fall in place. I have never really had, but I have always had the desire to help and advocate for others, and I know one day I will. Doing something good for others will make you feel happy that you forget your problems, or even that you are sad. You forget about your own problems because you feel such joy when you give to others. Remember, it's better to give than to receive. Having an unselfish heart, never being full of ourselves but just loving others, and when you do, you will attract nothing but good.

Why is it when we do good but people do us wrong? We do evil with good because what we gain by doing that is just hurt, pain, and resentfulness. If someone does evil to us and all we give is love, in return, either that person will change towards you, or they will just go away, and they were never meant to be there in your life. Why are people mean to others? Sometimes people hurt others because they have been hurt and they don't know how to deal with those emotions they feel or even speak about it, so they show their ugliness to the people they love the most, and even sometimes lose the people they love the most because they were too prideful to recognized what they did and when they did it was too late to fix it. When you break a glass, you can't fix it because you can try to glue the pieces, but the glass will never look the same; that is how it is when you break someone; you can apologize so many times, but the pain is so deep that it takes time to heal and when it does the emotions are not the same. You can forgive, but you'll never forget.

Stress is a killer. Do we stress? Yes, we do. Is it normal? Yes, it's the body reacting to a situation that we don't like or that will make us feel overwhelmed. It's not how it feels that matters. It's the way you handle the stress because there will be situations that are going to be out of your control, but you will be able to control it, and you know how it's the way you control your thoughts and emotions. Yes, it is easier said than done, and is it hard? Yes, I would be lying if I said no, that it wasn't, but what I have learned and continue to learn is that when a situation happens, I think and reflect, I think about what is happening at the moment, and I reflect how did this happen and how can I fix it, is there a solution. A Lot of times, when we run into situations in life, we want to run or hide or, like they say, fight for flight. We are so ready to fight the situation of taking ourselves to an ugly place. Did I ever do that? Yes, let me share a little if you haven't read my first book. My scars tell my story. Have I made mistakes? Yes, I even lost count. I have also hurt people I wish I didn't, like my mom, my kids, and my husband. I am not proud of the choices I made in my journey, but they were lessons learned. In those moments, I didn't know how to react. For example, when my marriage was in a place where, I threw in the towels many times because my husband didn't want to communicate. Because he would say it's not important. It's just a frivolous conversation, and it's not relevant. Those were his exact favorite words he would tell me, never beg a person, let alone a man, to communicate. If a person or a man doesn't want to communicate, then he doesn't find you worthy of talking to. I am not saying that every conversation is a good conversation, but when it means that it can save your marriage, then yes, you have to fight to make it right, or it's not a marriage anymore. You are just with a stranger that is sucking the life out of you and controlling you. Love should never hurt. Love is peace. Love is an emotion that keeps growing every day. Maybe in the beginning, couples might not be madly in love, but they will eventually get there. When you get there, it just keeps growing, and you know why because a woman is like a flower; it will only blossom and grow as long as it keeps getting watered. Never, never let anyone stomp on you or demean you. Know the warning signs. It can be a family, a friend, or your spouse, but you are worthy. You are a warrior. You are not a doormat, so walk with a purpose and with your head up high.

Self-care, what is this? You take care of yourself. If you're tired, rest, but never give up on yourself. If you need to cry, cry, but never suppress your emotions. If you're angry, don't take it out on your loved ones but write, and if you don't want to then walk or go to the gym, but never give up. You are a winner, not a loser. It's ok to feel tired and weak at times. We are human; our bodies send us signs that we need to stop or rest, and we ignore the signs, and then we pay the consequences of our neglect of our bodies and that is where our sickness comes.

Don't wait until it's too late. Our body is a temple. We treat it with care, feed it good food, nourish it with good words and lots of rest. We first need to rest our minds, you say. How can we do that well? First, we start by dumping out all the toxic thoughts and things that don't belong there and fill them with affirmations everyday, speaking positive things into us. Our eyes are careful what we look at or read, for not everything we see is good for us. Our lips speak life into ourselves, and others, for our tongue is a deadly weapon. We can use it for good or evil. It's our choice. Choose wisely. Our hearts let no one break our hearts or even let just anyone have our hearts, for not everyone is worthy of it, so be careful who you let in. It's ok to be alone, take your time. As you continue to read, we can trust in being alone and falling in love with ourselves. Our hands, or hands, can be gentle and used to pray for people, hug people, or just shake a hand and say you have done a great job. What have your hands done? Your legs. Our legs will take us places, good and bad places, but only you can tell your legs where to walk.

Just remember that we are always given signs in our life when we are taking the right direction or not. You know how because when we are on the wrong path, you will feel it, or people around you will feel it and warn you. People or family are not just in your life for nothing. They are placed in our path while we are on this earth, and some of them are like our angles looking out for us, but we just don't know it, and at times, we can get so caught up with ourselves or that situation that we are to blind to see that our pride gets in the way and next thing you know we fall flat in our face, but we get up we either learn our lesson or we just keep making the same one. Why do we make the same mistakes?

My therapist once said to treat yourself like you would want your daughters to be treated. That got me thinking. Imagine if I never broke the negative cycle of abuse and just settled, I am pretty much saying I am ok with my daughters settling with someone who would abuse them, and that's ok. I don't think so. It really made me really evaluate myself even more because it's hard for me to let go of my past and the people in it because it hurts, and I care. It's evident that they are cold, callous people in this world who just shut their emotions and don't show any emotions anymore and maybe even move on, well I've learned that instead of having closure, take that as an ending of that chapter, the cold shoulder or the silence of no communication for a while, just says it all.

There is no excuse for grown people to have to beg or go after a person or people who don't show any love, it's time to say goodbye and close that chapter and start a new one. Never beg someone to stay, never chase anyone, fall in love with you, and you will see the peace and freedom you will feel and you will begin to see doors of opportunities open when you least expect it.

CHAPTER 15
HATERS ARE GOING TO BE ELEVATORS

When you are down and defeated, no one pays any mind to you, but when you begin to shine and are full of love and kindness, most of all, the doors are open. Everyone wants to jump on the bandwagon. It's ok to say no; it's ok to be selective about who you want in your circle, I am not saying to block out your family or people dear to you, but keep it very humble and straight to the point. I used to think that only famous people had haters, but not so; just to be you, you will have haters because you have something they don't have. It can be a variety of things, but at the end of the day, they have enough time and are bored to hate on you; you just keep on walking, keep on shining, and let the haters elevate you. Well, here I am mid-year already, and it has been the most amazing 6 months of 2024, not that I haven't had some months that were discouraging. I had to hit the rock button to be able to say girl, get yourself up and wake up. Time is passing you by, and you can't get it back. My first book came out at the end of July 2022. I can't believe the impact it has made on many, and I most definitely can not stop writing. If this is what writing does, then I don't want to stop. I know it's not the easiest thing to put your mind to, but when you do, you can not even stop. From the moment I get up to the moment I go to sleep, I have something to do. I wake up at 4 am in the morning to commute every day to work and start at 7 am to come home at 6 pm and then cook, clean, pay my bills, hang out with my kids, read and write, and on top of that do online school, so you see when there is a will there's a way, where there is a drive and passion doors will begin to open, so don't talk about it just be about it.

Well, who doesn't like poems? I remember finding myself rhyming and writing poems about what it was, whatever came to mind. Some might say it's spoken words, but maybe we all have a writer in us. We just have to lure it out and believe that we can do this.

Well, here it goes, why do I think? How does this small round thing in my head work? Why does it hurt at times? I feel it's going to explode because I don't know how to control my emotions, but all I can say is I can't stand the pain. I want to just crawl in a hole or yet cut my head or bang it against the wall so it can stop. Why is it that it hurts? Did I cause this pain? Was it stress, I say? Was it you that gave me this pain, I ask myself, or is it that I am running and I don't know where to run, so should I just hide in pain, and in the end, the pain is still there? Why does my brain feel like it's going to explode?

Love, what is love? Love is an action word. Is it, or is it an emotion that we think we know for some? We love with our minds, some with our hearts, but in the end, do we know what love is? Love never hurts, love doesn't envy, love is not jealous, but most of all, it's long-suffering. Love: do we practice it, do we love, do we love ourselves, or do we expect love. Remember, we can't buy love; love is a gift, but some might not know how to give it or receive it. But what do you do with love? Love yourself first before you love others because how can we know love when we can't even love ourselves.

CHAPTER 16
TURNING YOUR PAIN INTO PURPOSE

Women, god created you so tender, emotionally full of love, to give this world children, but most of all, suffer but suffer because you care. Sometimes you give, and it's not reciprocated back to you, but you give; just know that I see your heart, and one day it will be given back to you, but most of all, never give to be noticed. Never give up because you want something back. Give because you love, and that is you loving yourself to love others. Remember, you are beautiful, you are a queen, you're a rose that never dies but just blooms and is full of life, self-respect, self-worth, self-dignity, and most of all, self-love.

Not every day is going to be sunshine, but you can be the sun, and the cloud can be above. As long as you shine, you will block that darkness away with your shine. Not every day is going to be a good day, but it is so powerful how the brain works but, most of all, how your thinking works, so you see a lot of us tell ourselves, why do I suffer so much or Why do I have bad luck in life because so many things happen to me but it's not bad luck, you want to know that secret it's the power of the mind thinking, if you change the way you think it will change your life that is also called the Law of attraction, I never understood what that meant, but after I read about it I couldn't stop thinking about how powerful it is and now I apply it in my everyday. This is how you start, and some might now see results right away, but it will happen if you believe. This is how I overcame a lot of my toxic thinking and speaking, but most of all, letting go of my past and loving myself, and I saw a drastic change in my life. I want to share the tools that worked for me, and I am so grateful that I still apply them every day.

What is it that torments you? What is it that keeps you from your joy and happiness? Is it you, or is it a person? Reflect on what you want to change and change it. Yes, it's hard, but it is not impossible. Every day as I woke up, I told myself today was going to be a good day, and whatever came my way helped me face it. Feel me with joy so that I can bring joy to others. If someone has negative energy, help me to love them. If I have a difficult week or just don't know how to handle struggles or financial help, believe me, those days many times, and at first, I wanted to give in and throw in the towel. When I felt I couldn't find the solution to a problem and I panicked with anxiety, I had to stop myself and breathe and tell myself you got this, and you will see how you will find a way.

My life was not always good; I had good, bad, and ugly days, and I had to learn to work with what I was faced with, but if I didn't learn how to speak affirmation into existence, guess what? I would not be here today writing this second book. It is vital that today and moving forward, you spend some of your time and reflect on what you want to change, but don't spend day after day complaining about it. You are wasting days, hours, minutes, and seconds that you will not get back, so use your time with caution.

Live your life to the fullest because tomorrow is not a promise to anyone. If you had one wish and one wish only, what would it be? Just stop for a moment and say this wish to yourself. Do you know that it is said that if you repeat or say the same thing every day for weeks or months, you will find yourself manifesting what you are saying, so be careful what comes out of your mouth? We can use our tongues for good or for evil. What are you going to use your words? Maybe some of us don't know how to express ourselves or how to speak positive words to ourselves, let alone to others. Well, that is ok. This is why god has allowed me to share this book and tell you that you are not alone. Just because you had a rough upbringing doesn't mean that you can't break the cycle; don't continue the negative cycle. Break it, and you will see the amount of change that will come out. I want to help women be free and feel how much freedom they will have and love themselves more than ever before because how can you love others when you can even love yourself.

Why is it so hard for some of us to let go of people we need to let go. Well, that was me thinking that I had to hold on for years. Though I cried, argued, and even got depressed. I always had hope, but was it really hope, or was it fear at the end? It was just codependency and fear of being alone. Don't blame yourself. This is just a sign that somewhere along your childhood, you were pushed to the side, ignored, or even felt abandoned, and just the thought that you will lose your security in the relationship that you spent so many years trying to fix is so toxic, this will only destroy you. If a person in your life is not uplifting you but tearing you down, then you need to grab your bags and let it go. It's time for you or that person to go. Don't ever beg a person to stay or change a person because they want to change and want to evolve every day, not stay stuck. You want to go forward, not backward, with people in life. Are you growing, asking yourself that question, and if you are not evaluating your life, why and why not? But remember, nothing is impossible. Only you can stop yourself. You may say I can't because people in your life hold you back. No one can't stop you from being you; only you can stop yourself. You have the keys to success. Remember, your dreams are only as big as you want them to be. What are your dreams, are you happy, and where you are, why or why not. Think For a moment, spend some time alone, and just write down the things you want to change and the things you want to see in your present and your future. How do you want to get there? You might ask yourself I don't know how to get there. First of all, it doesn't cost you anything. It's called discipline and drive. We can only blame ourselves for our actions. We have choices to do right or to do wrong. Let me give you a head start on how I start to do what I am doing today. I wasn't always this way where I dreamed big and had passions. I always depended on people and depended on what I was going to eat and wear from the person I married, and in a matter of seconds, he was gone from my life, and guess what? I had to act fast either I was going to be stuck all my life and feel pity for myself or do something about it. Do I have my moment? Absolutely, I do. There are days I feel sad, mad, and anxious, but guess what? All those feelings are normal. It's called life, but you know what I had to do is embrace them and say today you will feel mad or sad, but guess what? Tell it goodbye after a day or two. Go through the motions but don't stay there because if not, it will suck you in.

You are stronger than you think. Why do we give people second, third, or fourth chances in life? Women, let him or her go. Don't waste your time and energy on someone who doesn't value you, respect you, or build you up but just drains you and puts you down. Ask yourself what you are gaining by staying. It's called "Noting," and what are you gaining by leaving you are gaining your freedom and peace. The next time that person leaves, say goodbye and welcome peace and freedom. When god created women, he created them beautiful inside out. We were all created uniquely into this world, so gentle and peaceful and happy as we grew up in whatever environment. The world took us into a good or bad life, but god gave us the tools to live life, not just to come into this world and not do anything. I know some of us came into this world and lived a horrible life, even becoming something that we never thought we would become. Some of us could have even become addicted to someone or something. Here is where I want to talk about things that might be hard for some of us, and maybe I might not understand everyone's road and journey in life that had to endure but one thing I can say we all have a past, and we all have our journey good or bad but we can not live in regrets because you know why because that is your story to tell and share to others that have also walked your shoes, never be ashamed of your past because your past does not define who you are and will become remember that "Queen"

CHAPTER 17
DO YOU HAVE OR KNOW OF SOMEONE THAT IS SO TOXIC

Maybe some people don't know they are toxic but bring so much negative energy into the room. Although that person might not know it, he always wants to be part of your circle, and you just don't know how to cut that person out of your circle because you don't want to bump heads. I never knew or understood why some people are so toxic, and they can speak about almost everything or anyone but never themself. Why is that because they are bored, lonely, or lack confidence in themself, or maybe the same goes for misery love company? I can think of so many people I know who are so toxic, but why would I put their names out there? What I can say is that it starts with family, friends, and co-workers. It never ends. The calls never stop from different people, family, friends, or co-workers, and it's all drama and gossip. Friends, it's random when they reach out, but the worst it's my work. It never ends. According to the Bible, it tells us that a perverse man stirs up dissension, and gossip separates close friends (Proverbs 16:28). Change the way you think, and it will change your life. This is what I tell myself everyday or just change my way of thinking. Every day is a battle, just waking up and not knowing what our day is going to be like, but in reality, you can be prepared for the good and the ugly so that you know how to handle the things that will present themselves. When I think of myself years back, I know I could have done things differently, but at the same time, everything in life was meant to happen for a reason and a purpose. We can be the ones to say I learned from my past choices or stay stuck in the past. Life was never meant for anyone to stay stuck because we have to evolve every day and strive to become a great person and reach and climb to reach our dreams. Just because it's A dream doesn't mean that it can't happen. If you could go back in a time machine, what time would you go back? I would go back to my high school years. I can still remember it like it was yesterday. I wanted to be a model and also a nurse. Did I accomplish either? Nope, but even greater as a writer and author. You can write your own destiny. You just have to make the best of what the world brings and never settle and use any and every talent in your life. I know for me, it was money, and in life, nothing is free. You want to do something, there is always a cost, and wanting to be a model was nice, but growing up with a poor family, I had to be happy if I got a pair of shoes, but it's not about sharing a sad story but a happy one, so I say all this is to say never, never give up on your dreams, because where there is a will, there's a way. In our world today, we have so many resources and programs that we can apply for funding. It's about how hungry you are for your dream and your passion. Don't ever, ever let anyone crush your dreams. Remember, the person that tries to do that it's because they are dealing with something, so it's not your fault.

CHAPTER 18
WAKE UP WITH JOY AND GLADNESS

Before you even step off your bed on your feet, always know and remember it's a gift to wake up. We can fall asleep, and tomorrow is not a promise to anyone, so remember to live it to the fullest. When you walk out the door, you don't know you ' '"ll come back home. Always wake up with a grateful heart and know that we are all a work in progress. Yes, we all have faults and strive to become our best. We have the tools, our mind, our mouth, and our heart. Our mind is a powerful tool, we can tell the mind what to think and control it and not let it control us. When we live in tough situations, we feel like there is no way, and guess what? At the moment, that is how it looks like, but when we stop and pause for a second, we can clear our mind, think clearly, and evaluate the situation. Some of us don't know of people who talk too much but don't know when to stop or react because they think this is reacting impulsively. Who said patience is easy? It's tough, especially when you don't want to hear what that other person has to say, but I feel and believe it's the mature thing to do, think before you speak. It's having self-control. This is something you learn. Not everyone has this in them, and this is when conflicts start. The greatest mind and thinker is one who can speak but also listens. What does Webster's dictionary say about listening, the act of listening to something? It is so nice when you have someone's undivided attention. You feel in that moment that you can speak and express your heart, Never let anyone or anything block your voice because it's your voice. Remember how you cannot love others unless you love yourself. How you want to be treated, treat others as well.

CHAPTER 19
DON'T LET YOUR PAST DEFINE WHO YOU ARE BECOMING TODAY

Do you know what is wrong with this world today? Sometimes, we want to live up to the world's standards, and guess what? It's not what the world wants. It's what you want because it's joy, peace, your joy, and success. We believe that just because we have a past, we have limited opportunities, but that is incorrect. Yes, it's nice to be able to go to a great college and study a great career, but guess what? Just because you go to college is not what makes you smart; it is what you do with your knowledge and brain. Your mind is a powerful thing. There are so many successful people in today's world who didn't even go to college and live their dream life, it's your drive, your hunger. How hungry are you to see your dream come true? Don't talk about it. Be about it. Yes, you might say it is easier said than done, but no, I will never say it's easy because there are no shortcuts in life. Some of us have to go through storms and tribulations and climb many mountains to get to the top, but you get there when you don't quit; please, please don't quit. Just stop and rest and remember that there is always a price to pay for greatness., but it is all worth it. I know I am my worst critic; I always want things to look and sound perfect, and even though I admit I am not the greatest writer, here I am writing my second book. Not only that my grammar at times horrible, but guess what? That won't stop me from writing. When you love something, you do it with your all and with everything you've got, and no one or anything will get in the way of that with what you have. I know I don't have much in life, but I don't bring myself down because I always tell myself that whatever I face in life is only temporary and part of the process to get to where I need to get to.

Never stop being grateful there is always something or something to be grateful for. I can honestly say that I am grateful for my three children who were raised just by me and that although their father was not in the pitcher, I was able to be there and give them what they needed and be a role model to them and although I did make many mistakes they don't judge me but are proud of me of everything that I have accomplished in life. I am grateful for my husband. Although I felt that our time had ended and that our moment had come to an end, it never did. There was only a pause in our journey; we both faced many challenges that hurt so bad and took time to heal, but here we are today, fighting strong and heading to greatness in life. So many people will be very surprised how everything turns around for the good and what the devil meant for evil. God turns it around for the good. Always remember that you never ever settle, and always expect the best for yourself. You deserve only the best. I know that when you find yourself in a relationship or marriage, you think you know everything and you can fix the other person, but you can't. We need to fix ourselves first before we try to fix others because when you do that, everything else just flows. For so many years, no matter how much I tried speaking and praying for certain areas of my husband's life to change, at the end of the day, everyone changes at their own pace. Just be you, love you, and everything else will just happen. Some of us live trying to fix someone in our life, whether it be our spouse or a loved one when in the end, we need to fix ourselves and let the rest happen naturally, and it will come. Well, let us go back a few years back, to my toxic relationship, and even though this is not what I want to focus on, I want to give you a glimpse of my first book, how I overcame so many challenges and also how some of these stories you are about to read and true stories but first let me share mine. Growing up with a single parent and my siblings was hard, not having both your parents and your mother always working. There came a point in my life when I looked for love in all the wrong places, but also, there were people around me who took my kindness for weakness. Being molested by family members and not being protected by your parents. I grew up too fast and experienced too many things too fast for a young child. Well, I know that some might even think, where were the parents when everything took place while you were young? Well, first, I can say that it's interesting how people talk and question how, right now that my first book is out, I caught my family's attention, but I am glad I made people wonder and question as the saying goes, curiosity kills the cat, I guess I will let people wonder until they hear me speak or on a podcast. This second book is a new beginning and new journey for me because I believe that putting my first book there has opened a lot of doors to bigger opportunities but, most of all, healing and growth, not just for myself but many who are growing, elevating to the beginning and greater places.

I know that many can relate when we feel stuck. What makes us stuck? Do we choose to be stuck? No, we don't, but one day, we wake up, and time after time goes by, and we find ourselves in the same situation, the same nonsense, and we just don't know how to move from that, well this is how I had to move out from bad situations, did it happen right away nope, I wish it would have. So whether you choose to hang on to something good or bad, there comes a time when it's time to let go. This was my time. We are not alone. We are in this together. You are not reading this by coincidence, but it was meant to be at this time at this very moment. I believe that it's not just my time to shine but yours as well. You got this love, raise, and shine. Don't let anything or anyone steal your joy. Just flick them off like a bug on your shirt, and know that this is just the beginning, and any negative thought or word that comes your way or in your mind, say to it not today satan, just keep on moving. I am a warrior. I am a queen. Nothing nor anyone will move me with words because I know that I am becoming the greatest version of myself. My thinking is different, my words are different, and even my attitude is different. For those who hate me, just keep on hating because it's only raising me higher every time, and you don't even know it. Just come follow me not to hate but to elevate so you can walk into greatness on this journey.

We all come from many walks of life, and is it easy? No, I would be lying if I said this journey would be easy. I had to go through many things in life to be in the place where I am today. Am I contemptuous? Nope, I am still evolving each and everyday, why because my journey is just beginning. Although my journey has been challenging and painful at times, I know those were lessons learned, and I am still growing. We all are but let us not stay there because all we are doing is blocking the doors that need to open to great blessings. For those who know me, I have a big heart and am very giving, but some would say that I am too vulnerable or weak. They are wrong because there are not too many good women or good men out there, and when you find them, people don't know how to treat them because they never had good in their life. Never take for granted someone who shows you their heart, handle it with care, because if not they will run and never turn back.

CHAPTER 20
WHY DO WE SETTLE

Why is it so hard to put ourselves first? I ask myself this question so many times. There are those who will walk away from people who are toxic, and there are those who want to give them the benefit of the doubt to see if things will change you. You know what? They won't change, and the person keeps hurting you, and this is why they keep doing it because they know you will go back time after time after time. Throw away the trash. It is way overdue, and it stinks. Yes, it's trash, and it's dirty and toxic. We don't realize that we are going through this rollercoaster cycle of abuse and think it's ok and it's not ok. The fear creeps up, and you tell yourself I don't want to be alone, I don't want to start over, no one is going to want me with kids. I have good news. First of all, stop worrying about the other person's feelings and worry about yourself. If they cared, they would have never treated you and devalued you the way they did, and being alone is a good thing because you begin to value yourself, love yourself, know your worth, and never settle again. For some, it does take a long time to heal, and it's ok to take the time you need because it's better to remove all the toxicity in us before we start a new relationship. Some of us use other people as rebounds to cover our pain, and it's not fair to the other person. If you're done with someone, then be done for a minute until you have healed. Some of us don't give ourselves the time that we need to heal and to love ourselves. Why do we have to be with another person? For what codependency, why can we just love ourselves.

CHAPTER 21
STILL ON A TOUGH JOURNEY

This is what I am doing now. It's been quite a journey for me, but I don't want to speak about sad things or my story because I already have if you read my first book. But I just want to write about happy things and how we can be happy. Write your goals you think about; don't just think about them, but write them down and set the target dates that you want to accomplish them. Dream big. It doesn't matter if you're poor or rich. You can reach anything in life you put your mind to and never stop striving for it. Just be a go-getter; don't let self-doubt get in the way because it does. Time management is another one. If you're a busy person, then you know that you have to always manage your day-to-day. Let's talk about how you can stop worrying about what other people think or feel. They don't worry about you, so guess what? It's time to change your attitude and take back your worth and value. You do you and know your worth. Every day, you wake up with a can-do attitude and tell yourself today will be greater than yesterday, a new day new beginning. Yesterday, situations came and gone. Now, let's focus on today and what we want to accomplish today.

CHAPTER 22
WHEN YOU APOLOGIZE, MEAN IT

When apologies are no longer apologies, they are just I am sorry, but they are now repetitive patterns. If you hurt or someone hurts you and they are sincerely apologetic, you know, but when someone just says I am sorry and does it again, then that person was never sorry. They just think they can get away with it. Don't let there be a second, third, or fourth time of disrespect in a relationship or friendship. Yes, it doesn't happen only in a relationship but also in a friendship. There are toxic friends, too, and some of us need not only to cut a man or woman but also friends out of our lives because all we are doing is going in circles like a hamster, round and round, and it doesn't stop why because we allow it. Setting boundaries for ourselves, friends, and relationships. We can ask ourselves how we can do that well. I will tell you because I had to do it to someone I was married to, a co-worker, and also family members. Don't wait until it's too late to set boundaries; do it now. I know that when you are in a marriage or relationship, you can set boundaries to not allow that person to continue to do the things that hurt you but let them know it's not ok and express how it is affecting you if they care they will make the change, if it's a co-worker or a friend, set those boundaries to and letting them know it's not ok and if they don't stop then cut them, yes cut them, you will meet new friends, as far as your family members you can't cut them but you can set boundaries on what you will put up with and what you won't you decide.

A therapist once said what is a RED flag, I said Signs, yes, but is it just a sign or is it a sign to stop or yield. I said, stop, yes, but why is it that when people see red flags. Time goes by, but they continue to be with that person. The RED flag means STOP, like the stop sign on the street? If you don't stop, you will be hit something in a relationship or friend it will just blow up. So next time when you see a stop sign stop! Don't think or listen. Just stop and let go. It hurts when you have to let go, especially if you invest many years, but do you want to invest a lifetime of misery, hurt, and pain? You deserve the world. You deserve to be placed on a petal stool and never devalue your worth, queen! I will never say that it won't hurt and that you won't cry or feel lonely and depressed; go through the emotions and cry. Just don't stay there too long because, in my opinion, he doesn't deserve your tears. If a person shows you the ugly side, believe it and don't ignore it because it's alert, letting you know that it has opened another side of him that he hasn't shown you, and yes, we all have an ugly side, but it doesn't mean that we have to bring it out and treat our partner wrong. Don't get me wrong, there might be a moment in our life when we might have to defend ourselves from a stranger or a bad situation, and we have to fight back, but that should only be the time to bring that inner beast out, I call it lol.

CHAPTER 23
EVERY DAY IS A NEW DAY TO GROW

I never realized that even though you let go or cut tides from someone who changed you and left a deep scar, you think he or she is gone, but they are not until the healing is done. You did the first step by letting go now comes the healing. I didn't realize how much this relationship impacted me and my home. Also, this person is gone, but the pain and hurt are still there, and how I know it's because I see myself projecting myself onto my family and friends. I know healing and change don't happen overnight, but it happens one step at a time. Sometimes, we want to wake up one day and say it's over, and it's not. The person is, but not the fear, pain, and thoughts. It's ok to feel it's ok to take as much time as we need to heal, but we must do it and also let it go and not stay there. Never, never, ever be afraid to speak even if you can't speak to someone because of fear the perpetrator will find out. Grab yourself a journal and begin to release and let it out in writing. Write as much as you can; the more you release, you begin to heal, and when you are ready to speak, you will and have the courage to do so, but never be afraid because there is another you out there that needs to hear your story.

How do you begin to heal, you start by telling yourself it's not your fault and never, never live in regrets but just lessons. Beginning every day, as you awake and a negative thought starts, begin to speak a happy thought, meditate, pray, or speak affirmation to yourself. When someone tells you something negative, don't react. Just know that you don't know what that person is going through, and it's not your fault for someone else's actions because remember that for every action, there is an equal reaction. Never lower yourself to someone disrespectful, cut the conversation, walk away, or hang up the phone. As you fight back, you just entertain it and give power to the other person. Be a bigger person.....

Every day is a new day and we are also evolving and growing. Never be contemptuous, but strive for more, you got this. I know what it feels like to be codependency, and it's scary when that person is gone or cut out of your life. For some, we let go, but for others, it's a tug of war. You go back and forth with that person, but it will only get worse, not better. The percentage of those that will survive is slimmed. Never settle. You are beautiful, you are strong, you are great, and you will one day meet someone who will love, respect you, and be the king to his queen and also shower you with love. A woman is precious and beautiful and should grow every day being showered every day with love, just like a flower being watered because without water it dries and dies. The same thing happens with love and kindness.

CHAPTER 24
DON'T BE AFRAID TO LOVE YOURSELF

It's ok to love yourself, never depend on others' love, but love yourself first. Grow in your mind by feeding your mind motivational videos, books, knowledge, education, or just speaking empowerment into your body, mind, and soul. You are strong, you are beautiful, you are a queen. Don't wait for someone to tell you just know you are! I had to learn to love myself. It took several relationships to learn and accept that part of me, but don't wait. You don't have to be let down to tell yourself I am tired; just do it and do it now. Never give up, even if you are tired or tired like I felt many times. What to do when you feel like you don't have any more strength but just want to throw in the towel. Stop, breathe, close your eyes, and think happy thoughts. You can feel but don't react. Feel, but let go, no matter how long it takes, but breathe, but never allow someone else to steal your joy, demean you, or degrade you and make you feel like you're nothing. Cry if you have to, rest if you must, or talk to someone if you must, but never give up because you are going to make it a beautiful queen. You got this. The next page is a page to write down the things you are afraid of, the things you wish you could do, and why you feel you can't do them.

Things I'm Afraid of and can't overcome	Things I want to overcome

Look at what you wrote down, and if the good outweighs the bad, then you are on the right track, but if the bad ways the good, then this is where you start, and it's ok.

What steps can I take to get to that positive place that I want to be? How do I get there? Even if it's baby steps, start somewhere. Sometimes we feel that we will never be the same, I always think that leaving a negative person, my life will change, but I would ask myself how, when you spend so many years repeatedly going threw mental, emotional, or physical, but you will even if it takes one step at a time but you will love, just know you will. Just know that you will. I promise you, one day, you will look back and tell your story just like I did. You will no longer be afraid. You will no longer be afraid but strong and cry no more but smile and walk with your head up high.

Don't live in regrets. Why do we tend to beat ourselves when we make bad choices or, as we would say, should or could of would of right. We should have seen the signs. I could have made better choices, would the outcome be better. All things or choices we make in life are not just life lessons, but also they are meant to happen for so many reasons, but most of all, to teach us something, good or bad. Let go of the past, but embrace the present. In order to see what is on the other side, we have to let go of the past. We can't bring the past into the present, easy said than done right, but no, I know you can we all can. Think of the days, months, and years that we held on to something that caused us pain when we could have been on another level and grown in our life or just be in a happy place. I know for some, it takes longer than others but we all heal in our time. Just remember that whoever is in your presence doesn't deserve to feel your pain. They just want to give you love. Allow love to feel you and overflow that there will not be any room for toxic garbage in your present. There is no room.....

CHAPTER 25
WHY IS THERE SO MANY UGLY PEOPLE IN THIS WORLD

According to (Brogaard, 2020) says that abusive people want to have the feeling of power, especially when they feel powerless. They want to be in control and feel immense pleasure. They want to see others suffer. This is a sign of a narcissistic psychopath who feels pleasure in making someone feel helpless.

How can we embrace wellness and heal our mental health? What is wellness according to the Wellness Institute; it's practicing healthy habits, learning how to manage stress, and asking for help if you need to, but don't hide your pain and stress. Mental health can cause severe anxiety. We all face challenges in life. It's how we work in working through our emotions and mental feelings, don't wait until it becomes worse or out of control. There is help.

How do we manage self-care, eat healthy, relax, breathe, set our weekly and monthly priorities, practice gratefulness, being grateful for the things we have and for those we don't have. There is a reason and purpose for everything in life. Speak positive and affirmation, and always stay calm and connected to your mind. Every day, before you sleep and before you start your day, meditate and speak one positive word into yourself and speak it through out the day. An example I can recall is as I awake in the morning, I tell myself today is going to be a good day, and I repeatedly say that throughout the day, and I did. I did not allow anything negative to block my mind because I had only positive coming from my mind and soul through my lips so that I could give out good energy wherever I was.

I know today is quiet; it's dark, and I can barely see. Some days are like this, but I know that the sun will soon come out, and when it does, it will shine over every darkness that tries to consume me. Some days, we find ourselves with such anxiety and stress and don't know how to shake that off. When this moment confronts you, stop and listen to your mind, body, and soul speaking to you; it's crying out for help, rest, and calmness. Stop for a moment in times of challenges and trials, close your eyes and breath, and get lost in a trance away from anything and everything, even for just a moment, because remember each moment that goes by, we can not go back, it came and gone so embrace every moment good or bad because this too will pass. You're going to be ok if you don't have problems, then you are not living, crazy but true. Look at it this way: there are so many people in life who can not walk, talk, or are just stuck in a bed and wish that they could have some kind of normalcy, and some of us complain about what we want or don't have. The next time we find ourselves doing that, just remember you are alive, breathing, and a roof over your head. I know some of us struggle more than others, and I know it's not easy. I would be lying if I said it is. When you look back at your past, don't think of the regrets but of the lessons but also of how much you have overcome and where you are today; this alone should motivate you to never stop fighting but keep striving because, in the end, you got this!

CHAPTER 26
PAIN IS NOT SO BAD

Will my pain go away someday? Does it stop? These were the words I said to a close friend of mine. He looked at me and told me one day at a time, Thank you Kevin G. We all face challenges in life, and we don't understand why things happen. I guess I can look at it and say it will get better, if it might look far from my destination but it is closer than I think, it's not where I want to be but where I need to be at this present time. It's almost the end of the year, and here I am writing my second book, so excited and sad at the same time because I wish I could have the people who supposedly are supposed to be family support me or just be there for me, it gets hard to be alone although you're not, it gets hard because the people are there, but they're too high on the clouds living a fantasy world where all I desire is just a friend simplicity is what I look for but I guess sometimes in life no matter how much you search and cry out to people you end up alone, what does this mean it can mean a lot of things. It's time to realize that you have to be alone and do things on your own, cut the people that don't need to be in your life out of your path, and the ones you can't get rid of minimize the conversation. We have to learn how we can work with people so they don't work us up. Sometimes, when we don't take a step back to see why a person is being negative, they are just projecting themselves on us because there is something behind their behavior. You just have to listen and not react. Living with Mental Health growing up and being around people who had it not only made me understand it but also to understand others and not be quick to judge them.

My New year of 2023 was beautiful in the beginning. Never take that special someone for granted. With great responsibilities come great challenges. I was so excited to start this year on a great start, so I thought we can always strive and want great things or even expect great things, but sometimes you get several curve balls thrown at you. It's March, and I am still facing challenges. Sometimes, some of us experience so many challenges and wonder if it is ever going to end, I say? I am sick and tired of being sick and tired, but here we go another year, and not only good things happen, but bad ones, too. First I had a love one pass away, and I had to take a leave from work. Why do some of us not know when to stop and breathe, or should I say, when was the last time that you had a you day? For me, it has been 10-plus years. It had to take a mental break down for my body to tell me to stop. We live in a world that tells us if we don't work, we don't eat. If we don't work, the bills won't get paid, but what about telling us to take a break?

When was the last time you took a vacation? So you see, in this world we live in, we are treated like robots. We just fill in the role. If you have physical health issues or mental health issues, what matters to your employer is if you show up and do your job. Why can we just have a mental day, take a day to all get together to reset, refocus and readjust our mental health so that we can continue our week, that is a job that cares for their staff. We need to see this more in the workplace. Why? Can this happen, because it's not normal, you have issues outside of work; but then again you have those that are workaholics and think that they will take their jobs to the grave, when in reality, we are all replaceable, but our lives are not.

The following is an exercise:

Let's talk about the body.

- When you rest, your mind recharges, and you feel refreshed.
- You become more alert.
- You feel happier.
- You make better decisions.
- If you're hurt, it's okay to give yourself space but also set boundaries. Do you know someone who has been abused, whether mentally, verbally, or physically? These forms of abuse can harm your body, even if it seems like they won't.
- Emotionally and mentally, what can you do to avoid things that hurt you or make you feel bad? List some strategies.
- Do you speak up when you notice something unusual in your surroundings?
- Never let anyone demean you or speak down to you.
- Have you ever been bullied before?
- How did it make you feel?

Did you confront the person who bullied you? Stop and think about the above questions and write or

express what you can relate to, and how you overcame
it or if you are still struggling with it.

_____

_____

_____

_____

_____

_____

_____

_____

_____

_____

_____

_____

_____

_____

_____

_____

_____

_____

_____

_____

_____

The 8 Keys to Self-Love and Self-Care

- Plan
- Patience
- Purpose
- Passon
- Pampered
- Emotional
- Mental
- Peace

❖ What is your purpose in life? Do you have a plan, and what does that look like

❖ Are you patient with yourself

❖ Do you feel like you have a purpose? Why? or why not?

❖ Make a plan/goals and set expectations for yourself.

❖ What are you passionate for

❖ Do you have peace in your life, or what do you do for yourself.

❖ When was the last time you pampered yourself

❖ Emotional/Mental, taking care of your stress level before it's too late

Tools:

- Practice self-love, self-care,
- Setting goals
- Time management
- Balance your week

Examples of self-love/Self Care

- Love you
- Take a bubble bath
- Run
- Go to the gym
- Exercise at home
- Yoga
- Go out with friends
- Go to the Solon and pamper yourself

List some of the things you do or want to do and how you can get there.

1_____

_____

2_____

_____

3_____

_____

4_____

_____

5_____

_____

6_____

_____

7_____

_____

8_____

_____

My story and what Self Love/Self Care looks like to me.

Author of "My Scars tell my story."

Happiness is what you can do at the moment, not what you can't do......

CHAPTER 27
CHECKING IN WITH YOURSELF

We all have moments that we want to pause or have someone to tell us it will be ok. If you are not in a happy place in your life right now, check in with yourself. Tell yourself, why am I not happy? Is it me, the environment, my lifestyle, or my work. We all have choices in life and not all of our circumstance we encounter we have control of but what we can control is how we choose to feel, is it easier said than done yea, I had many people even therapist tell me go to classes to learn to deal with your emotion, thinking and anxiety but you know they are 50 % correct and you know why but the majority of time it's not so much to just give someone a bandaid and go on your marry way, there is so much more to mental health and as some that has suffer with mental health as a your teen and through out life, I know what it is to be depress, I know what it is wishing I was not in this world, I know what it is to have severe anxiety and have no motivation do do anything, not get out of bed or even want to be around people, believe me we all have our good and bad moments but some are worst then others, so I say all this to say is not to be ashame of mental health problems but embrace them and no that you are not alone and there is help, it's not easy to find someone to trust and even open up to so choose wisely who you allow to come into your life and tell them what you are going through, it can be from a parent, sibling, spouse, friend or a therapist but if a person can't sit there for more than a few minutes and then interrupt up or be dismissive then you are opening up to the wrong person. I say all this to say that when any person, young or old, at some point in our life, we have gone through a tough challenge or trauma. It's not about a one time that can fix a person, but it's being that friend or person that will never judge you and love you with all of your imperfections and tell you it's going to be ok when a person has gone through so much they are like a banana when we peel it before we can eat it right if not we don't know what's under so we take off all the layers over it to get to the good part of it and that is our heart, everything consuming us on top is so heavy that we can not even walk because it weighs so heavy, why do you think this is don't be afraid to say no, don't be afraid to say I will stay home today and rest, don't be afraid to take a vacation to give yourself a mental break, how can we function when we run out of fuel, fuel is our water, food, sleep, joy, exercise and peace. Can we honestly tell ourselves that we do this? I know I don't. If not, I would not be writing this today. As I write this book, I not only speak to you but also speak to myself. This year is not only a New Year but a year of transformation for many. It can be for all because we are in charge of our destiny, not a person, not a job or situation. If you are not happy, then do something about it. I did even though I was in a dark place, but I had no one to push me, tell me don't worry, I will pay your 3 months of mortgage, don't worry, I will pay your water so it won't get turned off or that your light would be shut off if you didn't pay, oh wait and tell your kids it's going to be ok I will put food on the table even you don't know how much you will have left to feed your three children, yet I was depressed, alone and defeated. I had to tell myself it's going to be ok even if you don't know. It's just speaking it into existence is what makes things happen. God said if you have faith as small as a mustard seed, you can tell the mountains to move. You have control of your thoughts, not your thoughts of you. You can stop what comes in. In the same way, you set boundaries for a person. You set boundaries for your thoughts; the same way they come, and the same way they need to leave. They can pass by and say whatever they are going to tell your brain and keep on moving negative thoughts. You are not welcome. I know we have difficult moments in which we don't even have strength but just give in. It's ok to not feel ok. Just don't stay stuck in that place. I did, and it was not pretty. I have gotten to a place where I no longer want to feel ugly inside or allow any thought to tell me that I can't do it, but I know I can. Whether you are a man or a woman, we all have a sad moment discouragement moment, just know this will pass. Write down what you feel and what you would like to work on and have had a hard time getting rid of what can you do to make that go away, A page to reflect.

NOTES:

CHAPTER 28
MENTAL HEALTH COMES WHEN YOU LEAST EXPECT IT

You don't one day wake up and tell yourself, I want to be sad or depressed today, It just happens whether you invite it in or not it just arrives when you least expect it, but guess what? Sometimes, it won't leave or refuses to leave, so like my mom always said when you overstay your visit in someone's home on the third day you will begin to stink, just like food left out. So embrace your sadness and depression, It's not always bad unless you hold onto it and it won't go away. Cry if you must but don't bottle it inside, and people will not want to be around you. I know there are different types of depression and different ways of coping with them. I will explain. Being depressed; if anyone tells you that, it's not true you might be sad because your not feeling well and people might think you are depressed and you are just having a bad day or not well so people need to know the difference between being sad and being depressed. When we are depressed, we can also be depressed and be ok, but once it controls us, then it becomes a problem and worrisome to the point some even lose their life. We don't want that, but Renee, you don't understand. I was molested, raped, abused, lost my job, my gig, both of my parents died, or I am in an abusive relationship. These are valid reasons, and we handle them differently. I say differently because some are worse than others. When it comes to self-harm or suicide, then yes, you need help or get help because there is. If you have had some kind of abuse, then you need to work with someone you trust close to you or a therapist but never feel like taking your life, or it's better not to be on earth because it won't. There is a solution to every problem. You are stronger than you think. I have experienced many of these things I write about, and this is why I mentioned some of them. Was it easy? No, do I have my moment? Yes, we all need a good support system, but never, never, ever give up. You are precious, you are valuable, you are greatness and a beautiful human, and you are loved. Just always remember that and tell yourself that every day. As I continue to write this book, it's a journey that I am living, and as I walk through it every day, I write about it because every day, we have a story for those who wonder how to write a book. We are all authors of our own story, and a lot of us don't have outlets, so journaling is a great one. The next thing you know, you wrote your first book. In this next part, I want to write about data on depression and also suicide that so many people ignore the signs and can't do more because people will never tell us that they are suicidal. First, what is suicide? It is defined as death caused by self-directed injurious behavior with the intent to die as a result of the behavior. (According to the National Institute of Mental Health). As crazy as it sounds, but ever since the pandemic we hear about it more today than ever before. According to the Centers for Disease Control Prevention (CDC), The leading cause of Death Report, in 2020:

Suicide was the twelfth leading cause of death overall in the United States, claiming the lives of over 45,900 people.

Suicide was the second leading cause of death among individuals between the ages of 10-14 and 25-34, the third cause of death among 15-24, and then 35-44, so you see, it doesn't matter the age it can happen to anyone, know the signs, always check in with someone when you are not feel well or check in on your love ones, I know we all have our busy lives but we can never be too busy to check on those we love.

CHAPTER 29
WE ALL HAVE A REASON TO BE DEPRESSED

If we all share the journey that we all have been through, we all can share of some traumatic events that we have been through, so no one is excluded, no matter the color, race, or class. Depression doesn't have a preference for who it picks. Can we have a choice not to be depressed? Yes, depression can consume us yes, but it's ok to feel depressed; just don't let it take you to a dark hole because then it is hard to come out of it. How do we deal with depression? Well glad you asked. Depression can go away on its own, or we can do many things, eat well, sleep well, and exercise for some. We need to be on medication, and it's ok if that is what you choose, but don't be dependent on a pill to make you feel normal or happy. Just always know you can begin by loving yourself and know that you are stronger than you think, and this, too, will pass. How do we get to that ugly place, our lifestyle we live like our environment? For some, we are homeless, have lost our jobs, are in prison, have lost a loved one, are about to get evicted, have our lights turned off, or do not even have food to feed our children, but remember, these are all material things and cares of lives and these all have a solution, but death doesn't. Embrace your challenge and kick it out because we don't have no room for it in our thoughts, home, our children's lives, and loved ones.

CHAPTER 30
THE FRUITS OF THE SPIRITS

If you have some kind of faith or know of this scripture in the bible, I see self-love and self-care as the following fruits, love, peace, joy, goodness, faithfulness, gentleness, and self-control. We can say that we have experienced more than one of them, but have we tried all of them? We can because if we practice all, we will find ourselves having a whole other attitude about the everyday cares of life and focus on the good things. How can we start knowing that there is a solution for everything when it comes to self-care and self-love, and that starts with taking care of our mental, physical, and emotional being. Find someone to talk to when you are feeling down, change bad habits, if it's eating badly, change your nutrition, and you will feel better. Most of all, we all need some alone time to take care of ourselves, whether it's going to the gym, going out with a friend, or just pampering ourselves. Make a date for yourself just like you do for everything else. It's time to make that a religious practice and make it a routine. Why is it so hard, especially for those who work eight hours a day or even overtime? Some of us don't take breaks. We put ourselves last and everything and everyone first. I am one of those who have done that all my life and it's hard for me to say no. It had to take for me to have a nervous breakdown for my body to say enough is enough, Renee. I felt like I saw a big stop sign in front of me telling me I couldn't keep going; I must stop and take care of myself before I can continue, or I will fall apart. Why is it that some of us have to get to that point to listen to our bodies? This year has been a life-changing year for me. I thought that going through all my trauma and challenges in life was it, so I thought, but boy, was I wrong. There was more to come.

CHAPTER 31
DIGGING DEEP

Digging deep into your young self and embracing the self-love and self-care movement. Self-love is crucial. It's all too easy to let the everyday stresses of life pull us down and cause us to forget to appreciate ourselves. Self-love is a time to invest in your physical, spiritual, and, most importantly, your mental growth. It involves prioritizing your happiness and well-being. Your needs come first—you're important. Before you start your day, remember that you can't take care of others if you don't take care of yourself. Pay attention to yourself; you are amazing and don't forget that.

Self-love and self-care are all about building self-worth and loving yourself everyday on your journey that is called life. As an eerie year goes by, never forget the lesson learned, whether good or bad. Take the good and embrace it, and the bad, learn from it. When we overcome a challenge or a traumatic experience in our lives, some of us will hold on to it, and others can move on from it. Stop and think to yourself why do we hold on to the past to remember it., to give it all of our power. The more we hold on to our past, it will block us from the blessing that awaits.

We are closing a New Year, and the New one is being welcomed in, what do you prepare for in the New Year. Are you one who sticks to your goals, or are you one who makes a New Year's resolution and breaks it in a few months? Let us not beat ourselves. Let us stop and think and prepare. What do we want to do differently, and what tools do we have to accomplish those goals? Start with baby steps. Some of us can make changes quickly, and for others, it takes time and discipline, but not impossible. You just have to want it. Set your goals as target dates, and always write them down. I have always learned throughout life that a dream is only a dream unless you write it down because it's visual. Have a planner but also a vision board, your three, five, and ten-year plan. Even if you don't have one, just create one. Even if things look impossible to see, they don't have to be; anything is possible, all it takes is speaking it into existence.

I want to change things a bit because although my focus is on self-care and self-love. I   want to share a little bit about how I got to the place that I am today. It didn't happen overnight.

These next few chapters are very personal, but life-changing for me, and I know that I am not the only one that is going through these changing experiences. For a while, I didn't understand if I was going through the guilt of all the bad choices that I made because, for years, I beat myself for so many of them, but I know

now that bad decisions in life are not mistakes. They are lessons that we learn as we grow and become the great men and women we are today. Maybe you never hear that because we are used to hearing. Why did you make that mistake

You will live in regrets. Next time you face a challenge because of a bad choice, embrace it and learn from it. It took me a while to really embrace myself. I spent several years beating myself and wishing that I could turn the clock. I know that if we could, we would, but we are all uniquely created differently, and no matter how many mistakes we make, there is always a reason for every choice we make, good or bad.

A moment of sorrow and pain as I get old. Not only do I get wiser, but I get so hungry to learn so much more, but at the same time I also face challenges that I wish I could make go away. Let me rewind a few years back. If I knew what I know today, I know, and many of us can agree with this, that if we would know the things we know today we would have made greater choices in life to prevent so much heartache and pain. I was hurt in so many different ways. Why do I share this in this book if it is supposed to be about self-love and self-care? It all comes down to that, but it all started somewhere first. Like they say, it gets worse before it gets better, right? Well, for a while, I had my fair share of mistakes, and also, I was hurt to the point that I thought I was not going to be able to forgive, but in the end, I was only hurting myself. You might ask yourself if someone hurts you and abuses you in any form or way, how can you forgive and make this pain or trauma go away. I will tell you how, I had to for a long time tell myself it was not my fault and to forgive myself because if I wanted to make this pain and hurt go away, I had to forgive myself in order to forgive others or people that have hurt us, some of us might never forgive people, you might say your crazy Renee this person did me wrong and yea I feel what you are saying at this moment, but you know what, all you are doing is giving power to that person that is no longer in your life, that person moved on and you are still holding on to that pain, and you can't move on, do you sometimes wonder why we are not happy, search your heart and mind, what are you hiding deep inside. The pain and suffering always has a root that it grew from, and in order for it to go away, stop feeding it and cut it loose. It has no purpose in your life anymore. Let's turn to the next chapter. Don't look back anymore. You are not going in that direction anymore. I know that I don't have all the answers, but I can only share what I have endured and overcome through my choices in life, and I want to let you know that you are not alone. Every day I wake up, I ask myself why I am here, I am going through another change in life as I get older, and I don't understand what it is. All I can do is embrace it and know that it will be ok, but most of all, I need to put myself first before anything, and so do you. Some days are good, some days are not, and the good ones might last the whole day or not, but I live day by day, and looking at life, I know that life challenges are only passing by, just like a boat in the river, it is just passing by, and we have to tell it hello and goodbye. The internal and external pain we face in life comes in so many ways; some are like a shower of trials, and some are like lightning. I don't know when it will come and how long it will stay; all I can do is always be positive and have support of some kind, always stay healthy the best I can, never take your health for granted or others, embrace your loved ones as much as we can because they can be here today and gone tomorrow. Our mind is like a wave of emotions. They come and go, but for some, it feels like the waves of depression or trouble never go away. I was there once; we all go through something, but we don't have to stay there. It is easier said than done right. One thing I have learned through the trials and storms of life is that we don't have to stay there, and if there are people that we just can't cut from us because they can be family members, it's ok. All you can do is be part of their family but not part of their circle. The family will always be family, but it doesn't mean that we have to live or be part of a toxic circle. Toxicity can come in many shapes and forms. In order to live a stressful and toxic-free life, don't let anyone or anything control you. We are our own boss. Remember only we can give permission for someone to take control. Ask yourself, does someone control you, control your every move? I know some of us can be married and the husband can be the lead in that marriage, but a wife should never be afraid to speak or express herself or in a relationship. Know the signs. We are beautiful human beings, and we should not feel like we can not love ourselves or need the approval of a person or someone to make us feel love. All we need is to love ourselves first. Remember that.

We do not need to please no one in any way, shape or form. As we walk in this journey called life, there are no shortcuts. Sorry to let you know that, but what I can tell you is that as we walk and preserve through this journey called life, it will get greater, you'll see. Just believe. You will look back and laugh and say I can't believe I went through all that, but that will be your story to tell to others so they too can say if he or she made it, I can too. Do me a favor, and don't give up. Coming from someone who went through severe depression and attempted suicide multiple times, well, I am still here and plan to for a long time. I know we all go through our sad moments where we feel like it is not worth living anymore, and it gets dark, really dark, but then the sun comes out, and the storm is gone. Don't turn out the light of your life too soon. There is so much that awaits you in your journey you just don't know yet because the present is a mystery, and you are not supposed to know you just have to take one step at a time.

Being a single parent and not knowing or having the resources I have today, I learned everything the hard way, like many single parents out there have, but for some even harder. Moms never give up no matter how hard it gets in life, and we feel like we can't carry the load anymore because it is getting too heavy. It will get lighter. Just hang on a little bit longer because, remember, this too will pass. We will not be in the same place the next day, next week, or next month. I went through a moment when I didn't know if I would get up the next day or if I would be able to provide for my family. All I knew was that if I held onto my faith everything would work out for the good. I serve an amazing father named "Yah-weh" who is sitting at the thorn and watching over his children, and if we believe he will forgive if we accept his truth and love, without him, none of this would be possible. It is only by his grace that I am still here today. As we say goodbye to 2024 and entering a New Year, let us not make a New Year's resolution. Let us just be excited about what awaits. Let us just be hungry for change and determination, and we will do it, and it will be manifested. We got this. As every year comes and leaves, let's turn the page to the next chapter and not look back but open the new door where so much awaits joy, peace, happiness, and prosperity. You don't feel it or see it, but it is right there. You just have to let it in. What is Love? According to Webster's Dictionary, Love is an action word. Many may say it's affectionate, a feeling, but love to me is maternal, and it's unconditional. Some say I have unconditional love for my wife or husband, but the only person that has unconditional love is a mother's love; no matter what you do in life, good or bad, a mother will always welcome you into her arms, but can we say that about people? People fall out of love, but a mother's love never dies. But in a relationship, love does. Men and women come and go, but there is only one mother and one mother's love. Share and value your mother if she is alive. If not, cherish your wife or partner. Even when you are mad, still love them because when that person is gone, you can't bring back the past. You can't say sorry you can't ask for forgiveness. Do it now. Love your loved ones while they are here because we don't know when or how long we will be here. Live today as if it was your last with love and happiness that everyone around you will want what you have because you walk with love, peace, and joy on good days or bad. Remember, tomorrow will be a better day, don't let stress suck you out of your years. Stress is one of the number one killers in society. Life is too short to waste it. I will be the first to tell you that.

Life is hard, and I have my really bad moments where I hate the world, but at the end of the day I know that this emotion or pain is only temporary and it was just leaving.

In this journey I am on right now, I don't understand what the heck is going on, and it's ok not to have all the answers. Just enjoy the journey, not the destination. Your journey is your process, we can not let our story challenge us; we wrote the manuscript so we can change our story. We can blame people for our happiness, remember, happiness comes within; don't let anyone control your happiness. You own it. Take it. It's yours; don't let happiness depend on a person. We need to walk with purpose even if we don't feel like it, not in defeat; no matter our circumstances tomorrow will be a great day. Challenge your story, don't let your story define who you are today but who you will be in your future. Remember, you are the author of your story, so don't look back. You're not going that way. No matter how dark your path you are walking in right now, you light up the way because the father is your lamp. Don't be afraid of the path you're on. He will be your road map. If you get lost along the way, he will bring you back to the center.

.

CHAPTER 32
THE PAST, THE PRESENT, AND THE FUTURE

My life has not only been a rollercoaster journey but also a transformation in the span of three years. Some will change slowly, some rapidly, but in this journey, you just have to fasten your seatbelt and go through the process, whether good or bad. In my past, I started with losing some and gaining some people in my life, but in this journey you will be on, there are only a few that will follow, and it's ok. I searched in all the wrong places for answers because I wanted to feel wanted and loved, but love was within. I just needed to embrace it because men and women will betray you, but betrayal will not only teach you a lesson but make you wiser in who your friends and family are and you will be surprised. As I walk in this journey it also taught me forgiveness and lots of patience.

Patience, I never knew I had. Fast forward 10 years today. I am standing tall, strong, a warrior, and with an attitude like I can take the world, preparing for the next chapter of my story. One step at a time. The past is history, the present is a gift, and the future is a mystery. How do I keep moving through this journey we call life? Several months ago, I started to not feel my body; I couldn't feel my hands and feet. I felt trapped and paralyzed, telling myself, am I being punished for the wrongs I did in life. It's been over 4 months, and my symptoms don't leave my body. At first, my doctor thought it was arthritis, but it turned out to be negative. I wake up every day hoping I can feel normal or asking myself, is this my new normal? Embrace it and move on right now. That's how I feel. Just go with the flow. I ask myself how can I feel normal, and how do I adapt to this new life. I feel alone and in the dark, no matter if I hear I love you, you are strong, you're awesome. Who are they speaking of? If you find yourself in a dark or lonely place, just know that you will be out of that place sooner than you know it. That desert will soon have water, that dark room will soon have light, and that storm will soon pass. Always remember you have gone through the worst in life, and this too shall pass. This is what I have to say to myself every day. Is it easy? No, it's not. Some days, I don't want to be here. It's hard to fight because you feel like you don't have strength, but when I look at my three children, I know I have to keep fighting, I know we don't all have children or maybe are in a place right now that you wish you weren't, but I tell myself, I am in the place I need to be even if I don't understand why, yes life is not fair. It was never meant to be perfect. Sometimes, when we turn on the TV or even social media, we see people that look like they have a good or even perfect life but that is not the case because everyone has a story behind all the riches.

How do you forgive yourself? We do it one step at a time. We think that forgiveness comes overnight, and it doesn't. I had to learn that to this day. I don't like making mistakes, but I had to learn that mistakes are not regrets but life experiences and choices. I don't have a time machine; this is my life, and I know that if I had not gone through this journey, I would have never written this book and the many to come, so if you are reading this book, it's because it has been published and you can relate. Remember we all have a story to write, it's not how you write it that counts, you either learn from it, or you keep living in your past, or you keep moving. It's ok to hurt, to cry, and get angry, but just don't stay there. Remember, depression is a disease that we don't need or need to let in. I know that so many have been on the path, and I can speak on this because I was once there; it's not fun, and from time to time, I have my moments, but I keep moving. Remember, depression is an emotion, and it can drain you and take away from you. If you or anyone suffering from depression, please reach out to someone. You are not alone. You don't have to go through it alone. I know what it is to go through depression alone. You don't want to tell anyone. You want to be brave, but most of all, you feel like you are all alone in this world and no one cares. I know not everyone might relate to my story, but if anything, be that friend that supports someone who is going through something, don't let them go through it alone like I did. I am at a point in my life that I am entering that I don't know what to expect. I do feel alone, sad, and sometimes happy, but most of all, I just live every day like it was my last and enjoy every moment, even if I don't know what the future holds. When I am frustrated or if I complain. I have to remember I am alive. I can breathe and walk on my own. Sometimes, we take life for granted, and we can complain about so many things, but what if you don't have your health? How can you live? You just live in the moment, but even those who are bedridden can be examples to many, so are motivational speakers and letting us know that if you have a heartbeat drive, you can do anything. All it takes is passion and your voice.

I know many have gone through losses these past few years, including me. How do you cope with loss? I will share my experiences everyone grieves differently. Some lose one, some lose many family members, and hate God, the world, or even a loved one. When we lose someone, we want to blame someone. It's ok to feel the emotions but remember we are temporary. So live life, don't be mad at it. Remember, we only live once. Our loved ones leave us too soon, but they are not gone. We will see them later. Don't say goodbye, say see you later. This is what I had to do when I lost my brother to gun violence. Everyone leaves this world differently. Old age, illness, or sudden unexpected death, I Am sure we can relate to one of them. Everyone mourns differently. Some cry, some yell, and some are angry. We all mourn differently, but one thing I can say is never to blame yourself for someone's death. No one understands why someone has to depart from our life all I can say to you is that, we are all just passing through some that spend a short time in our life and some a lifetime. I could never tell someone to move on from a lost loved one because some mourn for a little while, some a lifetime. It's different for everyone, but I have learned through losing my younger brother that I had to forgive myself, and also, every time I think of him, I think of the funny moment I got to live with him and my siblings. Those are the most memorable moments that bring joy to my heart and soul. Embrace your children, siblings, and parents because we don't know when life will take them away. Forgive them, never take them for granted, because when they are gone, it's too late. We didn't get there on time because of pride, hurt, or anger, so next time you miss a loved one who is gone, just think of it that they are on a long vacation and that one day we will meet them there. They just beat us to it. Embrace every day as it comes, good, bad, or ugly, remember to take deep breaths and breath. All it takes is one step at a time.

CHAPTER 33
IT'S YOUR TIME

How do you know? You don't. It's faith. You can't see it, but you can feel it. It's called hope. You dream, and you strive for your goals. It's called hope; never lose that, but hold on to that because hope is something that no one can take away, no matter if no one believes in you and your dreams. As long as you believe in yourself, that is all it takes to be you and reach the pinnacles of your dreams. Never stop persevering or dreaming. Just remember, when you dream, write it down. If not it's just a dream, a dream without actions it's only a dream. Make this year your year to accomplish your goals, even if it's just one, but that is one step ahead. Not every year you will accomplish all of your goals. That just means if it will take a little extra time to accomplish, it's ok. Just don't give up. There is no room to give up. I know we can think of many reasons we feel like throwing in the towel. I know I do. I left my job in the health care that I devoted 23 years to, and then I left, taking a leap of faith. Then, I developed a condition that I still don't understand. I don't know how I will wake up every morning if I am able to walk or be numb from my feet and hands, all my joints stiff in the morning, I cried the first month I was going through all this, but I remained focus and optimistic and just embrace every day as I awaken. I sleep, and as I awake, I take it slow and do my normal activities. I always tell myself this will pass, I will overcome it, and if I don't, I will embrace it and be happy I am able to wake up to a new day. At one point, I was afraid I would not be able to write, and guess what? My fingers got numb, but that didn't stop me. I will continue to write until I can't no more, I have a story to tell.

CHAPTER 34
STRESS IS A KILLER

Studies show, according to the Mental Health Foundation, that 16% of people have suffered some kind of self-harm due to stress, 32% attempted suicidal thoughts, and 37% of adults felt stressed and lonely as a result. We live in a world where we have all had some kind of stress, whether work, family or career. Stress can be good because it can motivate you, but for some, it can lead to severe stress and even depression. My experiences of stress, and I mean severe stress, pushed me to seek help because it was an uncontrollable feeling in my gut. I hated feeling on a day-to-day basis, and I was in a fight or flight mood, ready to defend myself and show my ugly side that I never show, but during those moments, I felt like I had no choice but to run and hide. I got to a point where my stress and anxiety got the best of me, and I didn't know who I was. I was going to sleep and waking up stressed. I was allowing people to stress me out and dictate my life and always worrying about if people were going to be upset with me. In other words, a people pleaser, and at the end of the day, people come and go just like jobs. We are all replaceable. I was always afraid to call out sick because I didn't want to let the patients, the doctors, and the management down, but the one that I was letting down was myself because I was crying out for help mentally and emotionally. I needed to love myself and give myself self-care and self-love. I didn't even know what that meant until all hell broke loose, and I couldn't take it anymore. I had a nervous breakdown and had to go on medical leave. For the first time in twenty years I chose me. I chose to listen to the inner voice, remember friends, our work will be there tomorrow, and if we are gone one day we will be replaceable no matter how long you have worked there. Your job doesn't care if you develop health issues. They act like they care, but once you don't come back right away, they are trying to figure out who will be next to do your job. An Office or Healthcare job is like being in a Soap Opera environment always so kind of drama, sad but true. There is always a new gossip story about someone, or they hate on you and try to make up some story about you that is not even true to get you in trouble. It doesn't matter how hard you work. At the end of the day, you will never be good enough, so I say this the next time you want to bend frontwards and backwards for a job, stop yourself and remember this is not your life. It just pays your bills. Your life is when you go home. Love yourself first, not your job. When you're gone, your job will continue. Wake up early in the morning with an attitude of gratitude, even if you don't want to before you get out our bed. Thank God for another day that he allowed you to wake up, that he gives you oxygen to breathe every day and not a machine. We have so many things to be grateful for, but the care of life distracts from the good things. If you think about it, what do we think most about throughout the day, the good or the bad I think the bad, at least I know I do, but I recognize it and change it so that I can have a more positive day. We can find so many things throughout the day to complain about, but all we need to do is remember that we might not be able to change the circumstances we are in, but we can change our attitude about it. There are things that we can change, and if so, then instead of complaining, change it if you don't like it.

The way stress affects our body can be very harmful if we don't know how to deal with it and use coping mechanisms' tools to control it; furthermore, I do believe that the way we handle stress can affect us in many ways, one can be in a negative way and another in a positive. The negative is because it can affect our psychological thinking. You can't think or concentrate and feel very foggy-minded. The emotional part of this would be feeling sad, scared, or even angry. The way stress can affect you physically. You will find yourself depressed, with loss of appetite, or even stress eating for some and having intestinal problems. Stress comes in so many ways. Stress can be nonspecific, pressures of life, or even chronic, where we feel we don't have control of our stressful situation. When this happens, your body automatically thinks about the situation and not a solution but is ready to fight or flight response and protect yourself in that moment.

The other stressor can be when it affects our minds because we can become foggy-minded. When you find yourself in a very stressful situation, you can make poor decisions and feel very drained and burnt out. We react out of emotions. Stress comes in so many ways, family life situations, work or just everyday experiences we go through. When we get a hold of stress and know how to embrace it and change the way we think about stress, I do believe that this will change the way our bodies react to stress. And not be afraid of stress, but be prepared how to face it and not run from it and become more stress free. Thinking about stress and reacting and having a coping mechanisium when stress occurs, we can have a greater outcome when we face stress in our everyday life.

According to the study of the (Peripheral Nervous System), it involves the brain and the spinal cord. When we look at other effects like the autonomic nervous system that is responsible for the heart rate, digestion, pupil dilation, and breathing, furthermore according to studies, the stress and hippocampus react to immediate stress, it can be beneficial, but when under stress it can produce a vicious cycle leading to permanent damage. This starts with the damage to the hippocampus, which increases cortisol. Another nervous system that can be affected is when we look into the (SAM System). This affects the nervous system that stimulates the adrenal medulla, which releases norepinephrine and epinephrine.

Stress has always been looked at as that stressor that can kill you, but in reality, we can embrace it and know how to face it in a way that we can control our nervous system and be prepared when we face a stressor situation. I learned that if everyone knew how to embrace stress and not run from it we would have less percentage of people affected by stress.

One situation I can think about was with my coworker and I encountered a negative conversation. I felt she was antagonizing me about the situation. I told her to stop, and she kept on poking at me. I made the mistake of reacting and yelling at her and saw a negative outcome when she responded in a negative way. A few days later, my psychological thinking of the situation was how she was going to be around me now. My thought process was in an anxiety mode. I felt like my body was acting upon the SAM system, because I felt my heart was beating fast because I was upset, and I was also nervous at the same time. At that moment, my adrenal medulla was reacting according to how I was made to feel. I know that if I had thought before I reacted, my psychology and emotional response would have been more positive.

CHAPTER 35
WHO SAYS YOU CAN PLAN YOUR FUTURE

It's never too late. Even if you have been through so many dark moments, you can create the next ones. Set goals even if they seem impossible; if you see yourself speak into existence, you will manifest it. Remember, whatever you speak, you profess. So I thought that this was not true but was I wrong. For some dreams, goals or dreams come quick, but for some, it may take a lifetime; everyone's journey is different, but there is nothing wrong with that. It just means alot awaits you on the other side. Just enjoy the ride, even if it's not fun. In the end, you will understand why you had a long ride. It's not for everyone. The Bible says many are called, for few are chosen. Don't rush greatness; remember there are no shortcuts in life, and for those who tried to take a shortcut, you will reap destruction or consequences from their action, so next time you get anxious and want to take a shortcut in life, remember to be still and know that the father has it under control. Your time will come when you least expect it. I have to tell myself that every day, even in my darkness moments. On this journey that I am now on, as I speak to you or anyone who reads this book. It's been so hard this year of 2024 as we begin this New Year. It is starting to be kinda shaky, financially and with my health, but no matter what, I can't give up, I tell myself. When I am depressed, cry if you have to, but don't give up. If I am mad, it is ok to walk, breathe, and exercise but go through the motions, but don't stay there. I know that if I can see my future, I will prepare.

CHAPTER 36
I NEED A BREAK, I CAN'T DO THIS ANYMORE

I need a break. I feel like my body is crying out for help. Can anyone relate? All these years, I thought that working and serving others was what I was supposed to do, but that is not true. I gave 23 years to the Healthcare Field, and don't get me wrong, I loved it and enjoyed it, but what I didn't enjoy was the drama and the fake people who pretended to like you and behind your back wanted to take your job or see you fired. 2023 was a year that not only did I go through a mental, emotional, and physical change, but most of all, I had to take a leap of faith and leave my job. It was scary, and I never saw myself doing that. I had 100 reasons not to leave, but one good reason why I needed to leave was. It was my happiness, or just accept it and just deal with it. It pays your bills. You know, I have met people along my journey that would tell me, Renee, I had the best-paying job, and I left it, and I ask why because my happiness and health are worth more than money, yes you need money to survive in life but at the same time when we leave this world we will take nothing with us remember next time you are worried about making money, it will all stay here, we came into this world with nothing, and we will leave with nothing. There are so many ways to be happy, but just remember that the material world will only bring you temporary joy, but it will still feel empty; the only thing that can bring you joy is self. If you look at today's social media, what are men and women doing competing, on how much money they have, their life is fake, it looks good on the outside, but they are dead on the inside, it doesn't matter how much money you have, happiness comes from within. Money helps to bring stability and comfort but not always bring you joy. Just look at the death toll of celebrities that are gone today, the cause of death, depression, abuse, or drugs. Why do I speak of this subject? Life is not all rainbows and sunshine; I know it is hard, and alot of us have been through the storm and hard. Believe me, many times you might have thought, what's the point of being in this world with so much suffering? Yes, that was me, but you know what kept me going was my three children. They are who I live for. We are in the year 2024, a year of ups and downs for some, but it doesn't mean you have stay there, I know it's easier said than done. I know I can't speak for everyone's story, but what I can do is encourage, uplift, and motivate anyone, just like I was motivated by many close people and people I heard or read on social media, yes, social media. Being the middle child was hard because I had friends but not many, and it was not easy for me to trust. In the end, I don't really have many friends, but what I can tell you is to also be you and never be a people pleaser so people can like you or follow you. Love yourself, and be your own best friend. What I mean by that is trust yourself, pamper yourself, go out by yourself, alone time with you without anyone telling you what to do, you do you!

CHAPTER 37
THIS STRESS IS GETTING TOO OLD

This stress is getting old. Am I the only one that feels that way? I felt like I was walking on STRESS AVE for all my adulthood. I felt like I was cursed or something. I know when you are walking in a dark place or just a moment in life where you are being shaped into the great person you are becoming, it doesn't happen overnight. It takes a lot to get to that place of greatness, and not too many want to pay the price, or if they want to get there, they want to take the shortcuts and believe you don't want to do that. You will later in life have to face the consequences of your choices, good or bad, and then you hear yourself saying, should of, could of, would of. Those are just excuses. I know so many people who have crossed my path and have used their past as their excuse because of the place they were currently in. Please don't ever, ever blame anyone for your past or current situation that you were or are in and I will tell you why. Each and every one of us has a choice to choose to do good or bad, to say no or yes. Your choice, your outcome. Always follow your gut and never let anyone dictate what you need or where you are going. Remember what I said in the beginning: you are your own author of your story, so stop stressing and get up and dust your feet and walk with your head up high because you are somebody and you are going places. Just claim it and see yourself already there.

CHAPTER 38
HOW CAN YOU LOVE WHEN YOU CAN'T EVEN LOVE YOURSELF?

This year, I had to do a lot of soul searching and really ask myself, am I going to put other people before my own happiness and see what happens, or am I going to let go and let god do what he has been preparing for me but he was just waiting for me to decide when. Do you ask yourself? I am way overdue for a vacation, a pedicure, or a manicure. Well, that's how I felt about love, peace, and happiness, I don't know if I am the only one that feels like that. I have always been a person growing up, and even as an adult always worried about what people thought. I didn't know when to say no because I felt guilty, but it had to take so much stress and sickness in my health to get a reality check and tell myself. I would rather be alone, happy, and healthy than be with someone who only cares about what they want and doesn't see the misery and pain the person is going through because they are too selfish to see it. Ask yourself next time when someone wants something from you. Can it wait? Can we compromise? If not, then you have to evaluate your friends or loved ones to set boundaries. Narcissistic family, friends, or partners don't know the meaning of boundaries. Yes, they exist, and if you don't set them for yourself or the other person, then you will find yourself feeling stuck that your life is not yours, but you are living for someone else. Beautiful queens never neglect your mind, body, or soul. I had a dream, and then I knew I needed to have a reality check.

As I awake, I tell myself I can't do this anymore. Why does this road seem so far but yet so close? Is this pain going to end, or is it just a maze that I can't get out of? I sleep, but I am awake because I feel like I am drowning but it's only a dream. I ask for help, but no one can hear me. All I can tell myself is one step at a time. This, too, will pass. I carry so much on my shoulders that when I sleep, I still feel the heaviness of the pain I carry. I keep telling myself this is not for you to carry; let it go before this anchor weighs you down. Remember, not everything in life is easy, and some things take time. This is why I say one step at a time, but remember, when things begin to sink and get toxic in your life, that just means it is time to throw out the trash. It's getting old, boo. All it takes is one step at a time.

CHAPTER 39
MY JOURNEY HAS JUST BEGUN

I don't even know where to start, but here we go 2023 was the year my new journey would begin because of the leap of faith I was going to take, and that was to leave my employment of twenty-five years. What was I going to do or survive? I had to tell myself I wouldn't know unless I tried, and if I didn't, I would have then wonder what if I would have not taken that leap of faith, but I am glad I did because here I am in 2024, and only but amazing things, doors and people have come and continue to come into my life that I didn't expect, but first let me rewind a year back before all this happen. Those who read my first book know that I come from a tough upbringing and challenges throughout my life, 2023 was a tough year because I was trying to make a relationship work that was broken and picking up all the pieces that was were once shattered, thinking that I could fix it. I was wrong. What I needed was to love myself for all the hurt and pain that I was suffering deep inside that no person or man can heal but the father, I was placing a bandaid on all the past hurt, and I couldn't get past it or even forgive as much as I wanted, sometimes in life we want to fix people, but in reality the one that needs fixing is yourself, with loving ourselves first, caring for ourselves and healing, and sometimes the inner you is crying out for healing and love, and we just put another relationship on top of Another and at the end, we are just right back to the beginning hurt. I know for some, we need to be in a relationship, and I am not ashamed of that because meeting someone along the way of your healing journey is a good thing and supports you along your healing process. Just remember that if their motives are about them and they don't understand your healing journey, then they are in for the wrong reason. Well, as I was going through my sickness, and when I say sickness, I mean from head to toe, my migraines got worse, I started to feel so depressed, and my whole body began to feel so much pain. I didn't know what was happening to me, and I top of that, I was worried for a man that all he cared about was himself, but again, this book is not about him but about my journey, so let's continue. There were days I couldn't even get out of bed because the pain was so severe I thought I was cursed or someone was doing some witchcraft on me. It was bad. I couldn't take it, so I reached out to my doctor to find out that she would scare me and tell me all these ugly diagnosis. She said you might have lupus, fibromyalgia, arthritis, osteoporosis, or maybe just going through menopause. Well, long story short, I have none of those, so now she wanted to put me on a medication that would give side effects of psychosis. I am already crazy, lol... I couldn't, so I did my own healing journey, and guess what it worked? Fast forward to January 2024. New Year's was a deal breaker. This was my last encounter with my ex, and I knew then that I did not want to spend my future with him. Fast forward to today, I have never been so happy, I prayed from every demonic force weighing me down so heavy and sucking the life out of me, but my heart, mind, and soul that has always had faith and that is what can't stop the father, and I am so grateful for my faith and prayer, that kept me and even though I knew I wanted out and I didn't know how, but I am so happy I didn't have to do anything but pray, and there is power in prayer and he walk right out of my life the best thing ever. I only wish the best to people that have come and gone much love but it was time to take out the garbage. It was stinky, much loved …. When one door closes, another one opens, and that is what happens, and it continues to. I am going to graduate from community college with an associate in Psychology, An Associates in Sociology, an Associates in Liberal of Science and also an Associates of Administration of Justice. To add to that, I earn so much more certificates in human trafficking, HIV awareness, and the Futuro Health MA program. Heading to a UC College, fingers crossed, I applied to three of them to be announced in 2025! So if that is not a blessing after blessing, I don't know what is. This to me, is self-care and self-love. For once in my life, I had to tell myself I needed to love myself and stop giving.

It's time to give to yourself; you are strong. You got this, Renee; you are more than a conqueror. I am a warrior, queen. Never let anyone tell you you're too old to achieve goals in life or think. Because you have kids, I can't go back to school; you can do anything and everything; it starts with believing in yourself. Where do you start? Start with you, love. You take care of yourself first, and if no one likes it, oh well, cut them. New and greater people will come into my life. I was not expecting the people that have come into my life but I am beyond grateful. I want to start by acknowledging my daughter Crystal. When we moved to our first home back in 2017, she went back to school, and she encouraged me to go back. I started with nursing, but it got hard because I was working full-time and I couldn't keep up with the classes, but I didn't stop there. Here we are today, about to walk the stage 2025... I don't know what the future holds, but I know that I want to do amazing things, and travel can't wait to do it with the people I love so much. Remember, our jobs are replaceable, and we only live once. Take care of yourself first before you take care of others. Remember, you are amazing, and you got this. One thing that this chapter of my life has taught me to not look back because I am not going that way. If I do, it's to remember how far I've come. I have changed my whole lifestyle, and everyone has their own way of dealing with challenges or stress. Mine is prayer, meditation, gym, and music. It's so amazing. I feel so much peace and harmony; I have my moments of discouragement, and I just rest and tell myself this, too, shall pass. The Bible says you will know them by their fruits, all I want is to love and give back, to let people know that there is a light at the end of the tunnel. If you are in a place of darkness just know you are not alone, I promise you it will get greater. I guarantee you, I know what it feels like when all the world is on top of you or when you feel stuck in your journey, and you don't know where to go from here. You got this boo you can do this. I want to speak to those who were told that they can't do this or Maybe have low self-esteem because no one believes in them, but guess what? I believe in you. You are amazing. you are a warrior, queen or a king. Yes, I speak to all, not just women. No one is excluded; I speak to all. We all need encouragement, we all have challenges, and I know it's not easy, even for men. My son had to grow up without his father, and I had to step in to be both, and it was very hard. I wish I could have done more, but I know that I can say I am grateful for the man he has become and the journey he is heading, so if you don't feel that people don't get you, you are not alone. I know how that feels. Sometimes in life, you have to walk alone to get to where you are heading, and that is greatness. and sometimes not everyone can walk with you, and it's ok because, along this journey, the Father will bring the right people into your life who will love you and support you and who are meant to be with you. Don't be afraid to let them in. I felt afraid to let people in my life after all the ugly moments in my life. I cried and told myself, will I ever be in a good place? Will I ever love again? Shut the doors of my heart, and it takes time to open your heart again, don't rush, start with loving yourself first and know that your time to truly love again will come, you cannot rush love. Love is patient, how can you love someone, when you can't love yourself, remember love starts with you not a person. In life there will always be bumps in the road but just remember to never give up and take one-step at a time. There will be moments where you need to stop and rest and even take a break, listen to your body what it is crying out for. Always remember you first don't let stress get the best of you, I never knew that stress can really take over your mental and physical health. The statistics are so high in America today. According to the American Institute, 5 out of 10 people have stress, which is 75%. Stress comes in so many ways, but there is also good stress, like exciting news, having a speaking engagement, or receiving an award. When it comes to the worst stress, you will know, and if you know, at least recognize that it's not normal when your body is speaking to you. It starts by not sleeping. It's so important to rest our bodies to recharge at night so that we can feel refreshed. When we don't sleep, we get so irritable and in a bad mood. Even our performance shows it in our work. Once it gets really bad you will feel sick physically. Your job can be a stress trigger, a person can cause you stress, a relationship, money and so much more. The list goes on: what is your struggle and how do you deal with it. I had to check myself and tell myself I couldn't do everything. I couldn't help everyone. First, I need to help myself, balance my daily duties, time management, and delegate if I can at work or home, but remember to take a break first!!!!!! Remember, it's never too late to start. I don't know what you are facing or what giant you are fighting in your life, but just know you can beat anything; just go back to the center and tell yourself, you got this, and tell stress you don't belong in my life, or people that don't serve you must go, don't let no one stop you or block your blessing that awaits. I became such an ugly person inside. It made me sick; I became this miserable, unhappy person, and I wanted the old me. I came out of the hole I was hiding, and I came out stronger than ever, and so can you. Love you, love you, I will continue to do it.

CHAPTER 40
BECOME A GREATER YOU

I always thought that I would just live to suffer because I couldn't remember good moments in my life, but only the one's when I became a mother, not my marriage because I got married for the wrong reasons, I look at this: the greater the calling, the bigger the fight we have to go through because our reward is waiting, there won't always be rain, you will have sunny days to and get to that beautiful rainbow that will shine when you get to the other side, remember you will win the race maybe it hasn't started because there is work to be done in self, search within yourself, and you will see and hear that inner voice tell you what you need to do. Great moments will come, you will see no one will be left behind, and you have the keys to success and happiness only you and no one else. You just have to open all the right doors and close the ones that don't serve you anymore, you got this. Remember to breathe when things get overwhelming and the days feel so heavy and hard and smile and tell yourself you are ok. The mind is so powerful. Your thoughts are powerful, but not all your thoughts are good. Our thoughts can control our actions, and when we feel that we can't overcome the trials we face so much, we need to take a shift in life. What I mean is that we need to speak to our ego and just smile and say no, you don't control me. If you want to live happily and live a happy life and live it to the fullest, shut that ego up when it wants to tell you what to do and just love, be happy, live in the moment, and don't worry about what tomorrow brings, let it just come and live for today like if it was the last one.

When we spend so much worrying about the cares of life, we are eating away every moment of our being that we can not get back. Next time when you get mad, or someone gets you mad, think before you react. There is so much power in our thinking, so speak to it and remove the negative thinking, and tell it goodbye. It has no room if you feel like you can't focus. Remember to breathe and release, readjust, and restart. Let those thoughts sail away like a boat passing you in a river. Tell it goodbye; you came, but you must leave. Embrace it for a moment and let it go. Let go and let god do the rest. Some might not believe in god, and I can't tell you who and what to believe in, but whatever works in your daily life, for me, it's god and meditation, but remember you are not alone. You got this. If not, you would not still be reading this far, and if you have, I am so proud of you. I know that when we are in a dark place we can feel like there is no way out, and there are people that love you and want the best for you and want to see you shine. Growing up and not having my family support was hard, but I had to tell myself I could sit here and cry about it or do something about it and do it for you and no one else. Whatever it is in life you want to succeed in life you can do it. Never underestimate yourself, I lived undermining myself for years, or I should say all my life, and the moment that I believed in myself and the capabilities I had in me, I had to let them out because they were cries to be released and I am hungry to do so much more, don't stop and never be satisfied until you know you have reached your goals and passions.

CHAPTER 41
HOW DO YOU START? START WITH FORGIVING YOURSELF

I asked myself many times why I have to forgive myself and not just forgive others, and it doesn't work that way. Although we can say I forgave you, it doesn't mean you forgave. When something continues to resonate, and you can be around that person, then you truly have forgiven that person. People who say they forgive but have a tenancy to throw the past at people who hurt them it's a projection of themselves that they are holding onto the past. If that person has moved on and is no longer in your life, then why are you hanging on to that person when they are no longer in your life? It's like carrying unnecessary rocks in your bag. Throw them one at a time so your bag can get lighter until your bag is empty. When people walked out of my life, or at least the last person that did that was my ex-husband, I still wanted to hang on because I said, did I do something wrong? Could I have done something different to make it work? The answer is no because when the story gets old and repetitive, then we have to start a new story in our lives. And that is what I did, and I couldn't be happier. I started praying and meditating, which I had stopped for the past 10 years because my life revolved around my past marriage. I never took care of myself; I always gave, and nothing was given to me. I was sucked dry with no strength to hang on. It wasn't easy to say no to people at times because I have always helped people all my life, and I didn't know how to take care of myself, and here I am today, self/care, self-love, affirmations, meditation, and prayer is something I had always done, but I had stop but now I find myself praying like I have not prayed in years and once again, applying it into my daily life today. Where do we start? I am glad you asked me to start small, and what I mean is love you first, listen to your inner voice, and what is your inner child telling you to do. Is it telling you to rest, eat, exercise, pamper yourself, or just be still? We all have daily desires to begin treating ourselves, and it's ok to say no to other people, you first remember that!

CHAPTER 42
STOP LETTING OTHERS CONTROL YOU

Controlling can sound strong but being controlled can come in many ways and many factors. Controlling can be someone controlling everything you do and say, or you being even controlled by your own addictions to life, what is controlling you today. Many of us can think of something or someone that has controlled us in our past or in the present. If you feel you are in an abusive relationship or have been or are in one, please reach out to someone in your community. There is help; don't feel stuck or be stuck. The first moment I felt I was being controlled was the first time I wanted to divorce my husband, and he didn't want to let go. He did things and said things that put fear in me. I told myself if you can't beat them. Join them. I was sacrificing my happiness because I didn't want to go through the fight or trauma of the what if he became vindictive and tried to take everything from me. One day, two years later, he emailed me and told me I was picking up my clothes and belongings. He didn't say why, but I knew at that moment that this was it.

I told myself I could sit here and cry and go after him or rejoice and say this is my freedom out of this marriage. Don't get me wrong, I don't hate him; I have a love for him, but as a person, I only want the best for him and hope that one day he can find someone that he can connect with. This taught me I either continue the cycle or break it once and for all, and I did. I filed for divorce, and doors began to open like never before, blessing after blessing. This had to happen in order for me to move to the next level for something great awaiting on the other side. Never ever feel that you will never be happy again if you leave a toxic relationship that is a lie from the pit of hell. The grass may not always be greener on the other side, but how do you know unless you take that leap of faith. Love yourself first.

God will put people in our path to teach us a lesson, but also we can learn from it and move or stay and let the cycle continue all over again. Don't be afraid of change; change is hard, but it is also good. Never get comfortable with anyone because we are only barrow, are only here on earth temporarily, so love yourself first and then love others, uplift and encourage others, and don't control. Give people space when they need it so that they, too, can give you space when you need it as well. You got this. Your time will come, or it is already here, but are you ready for the shift of a lifetime? Remember, don't listen to the ego telling you that you can't make it in life or go to the next level of your journey because you can, but you have to believe that you can because what you manifest will come, so be careful what you say and whom you say it to.

CHAPTER 43
WHY DOES IT HAVE TO HURT SO MUCH?

Pain, what is pain, physical, emotional, or mental suffering? Why would we want this right? We don't always look for it. Sometimes, it finds us, and when it does, it can be temporary or long-term. Healing from pain can take a season or even sometimes a lifetime, but the sooner you get rid of it, the better. Embrace the pain, but let it go. Don't stay stuck there because time will pass you by, and then it's hard to move on, and you will then look back at life and live in regrets, and that is what we don't want never live in regrets but look at them like life lessons and move on. You are not a victim but a warrior. Don't ever deal with pain on your own, even if you don't have someone close. Look for a healthcare provider if you need to, but you are not alone. Remember that you don't have to endure your pain alone because this, too, shall pass. If we didn't face challenges, trials, or our own giants in our lives, how can we move forward in life and grow? Life is not easy. It's not supposed to be easy; not everything is handed to you. It's earn some good things and some bad, take what is good and begin to let go of the bad. Just remember, when your ego is telling you to do or to feel something negative, speak to it and tell it, not today. Today is my day, and I will shine and walk in victory and not in defeat.

CHAPTER 44
THE FOUR THINGS THAT STEAL YOUR JOY

The Bible says in Philippians 4:4 Rejoice in the Lord always delight, yourselves in him. These are just four, but here are some many things that can rob us of our joy and I am sure we can all think of many of those things. The Bible also says that the devil comes to kill, still, and destroy John 10:10. What is stealing your joy today?

Before I say the four things that can steal your joy, I want to share a short story of what was robbing me of my joy. Eight years ago, I fell for a person in prison, and I thought I loved him and I ended up marrying him in prison while he was serving his time. Everything was amazing, although I was sad because I couldn't physically be with him but I was in my honeymoon stage for the first two years of that relationship. Well, you have heard that sane that you won't know a person until you live with them. Well, that is not true. For me, it was the trust and the blindness of the red flags that I didn't want to see, but everyone else did. Fast forward ten years later, this marriage became so toxic to the point I ended up sick in the hospital many times for elevated high blood pressure and depression. I felt lonely, discouraged, depressed, and stuck, but most of all, I didn't know how it felt to be happy anymore. Four things that will rob you of your joy.

- Trauma
- Toxic relationships/ Friendships
- Drugs
- Stress
- Depression

I will never forget the trauma. I thought that I was never going to overcome it, but little did I know that I had the keys in my hands, and that was to say, boy, buy, and the day I did, peace of mind, body, and soul came upon me, not knowing that all this time I had the answer, it's like I was holding on to pain, and all I had to do is letting it go for that door to be shut and a new one's to open. Remember, we are sometimes the ones who are blocking the blessing that awaits us on the other side. A toxic relationship doesn't always have to be a relationship. It can be family and friends, so choose your friends wisely. And, of course, we can't give up on our families, but we most definitely can set boundaries. Drugs How many know of someone who does or has done drugs? Maybe they don't want to, but maybe that is their outlet. Because of the trauma that they might have gone through in their life, they always know that there is always a way out. Never feel ashamed to reach out and get help. There is always help. Stress is the number one killer, control it, don't let it control you. When it comes to embracing stress, just don't let it stay. Stress is only temporary; it's not there to stay only if you allow it. America suffers so much stress, and for some, it can kill us. It almost killed me. There is good stress when we are striving for something good in life, but when the bad stress comes, just let it pass by and say see you later.

CHAPTER 45
IT'S YOUR TIME

How do you know if it's your time? Oh, you best, and I believe you will know. First of all, you will not question yourself because you know that when you are where you need to be, you will be in a peaceful and joyful place, people will begin to attract positive people into your life, and the door will begin to open you will begin to have a clear picture where you want to be and where you want to go there is no room for doubt. Anything or anyone that tries to get in your way, you will cut them out of your life, and your circle of friends will get smaller, but new ones will begin to knock at your door. The shift will begin to happen, but are you ready to walk through it? Don't be afraid of what lies on the other side. Some of us don't know how change feels because we have been so comfortable with routine, but some of us are so unhappy and just getting through life and expecting a miracle to fall from the sky, and guess what? It won't happen, the train of opportunities will come, and you will miss that train because you were sleeping. We missed out on an opportunity of a lifetime. Will it happen again? Yes, or maybe not. Don't be afraid to take that leap of faith. How will you know if it will work unless you try? Don't look for the easy way out. It is always easy, and

163

faith is hard but not impossible if you just believe. Start by believing in yourself and then everything else will just fall in place. You will see, I promise you. Focus on your journey, not your destination. In order to get to your destination, you must go through the process of your journey. It's not easy when you're headed to greatness. It's not supposed to be easy. Just get on the ride and just remember that there is a destination to reach. The bumps and blows that will be thrown at you are just part of the journey, just remember that everyone that tries to mess up and interrupt your puzzle is not meant to be in your journey. Just pick up the pieces of the puzzle and put it back together. This puzzle is untouchable. Set your standards and values. Mistakes are supposed to happen, and how can you reach your destination? There is no free pass. Remember to turn your pain into purpose, you got this!

CHAPTER 46
WE ALL COME FROM ASHES

We have heard from one place or another that we were born from ashes and will go back to ashes. When I look at the analogy as life, we come from a tough life, abusive, addictive life, or unpleasant one. What do you do? Do you stay there and live a miserable life, or do you bury it and say goodbye and never go back to it? Yes, when someone gets buried, you come to their grave sight, but when you bury bad memories, you bury them, and they only become memories. They are not there to haunt you but to always remind you of how far you have come. Don't keep visiting your past. It is called the past for a reason. It came, and it's done with. Dust your hands and feet and say to it goodbye; you don't belong here anymore. The past is your story and not your present, and it will never dictate where you are heading. It will only serve you as a reminder of how far you have come. When we are hurt and come from a traumatic upbringing, and we know nothing but survival, we are always in a fight or flight mode, and that is all we know. Our trauma feels like an eternity. I have been there so many times that I felt I was cursed I felt like I couldn't catch a break. I felt like every year, I was faced with another challenge or another blow in the face, but it was to prepare me for what was coming: the good, the bad, and the ugly. Guess what? I made it, and I continue to make it, and so can you. I don't know what journey you are in right now, but whatever journey you are in, don't quit. It will get better, I promise you. It's so easy to quit and hard to fight, but just like what we do when we want something, we fight until we get it. That is how life is to you. Want to be in a greater place? Guess what? It won't come unless you fight and you speak into existence.

CHAPTER 47
PEOPLE, PLACE, AND PLAN

People come and go, and some even don't want to leave our lives. How do we know which ones to keep in our circle and those we say goodbye to? Is it easy? No, but when you are going on this journey of success and prosperity, not everyone can follow. A few can sit with you, and others will just watch from afar. The places you are going to you might know or plan, but there are those places that are unexpected but are open opportunities that will come in this journey. Think big even if you don't know how you will get there, but just envision yourself already there and speak into existence; when you least expected, it will come, and then you will look back and say to yourself, how did I get here. You did it, yes, you did it, and all by yourself, and all it took was drive, ambition, and passion because you never stop believing in self. How can I do all this well? I am glad you asked; the way I start my plan and I am still learning, do not worry, there is no right or wrong way to plan, just plan. I start with prayer, meditation, and affirmations every day. Next, a journal to write down goals, dreams, and accomplishments and set dates. Don't just dream, but write it down to make it happen; if not, they are only dreams. Set realistic goals; don't tell yourself I want to be a millionaire in a week. Be realistic with your goals, and if your goals require you to go back to school, please do, always know that knowledge is key and power.

CHAPTER 48
DON'T EVER FORGET YOUR INTEGRITY, PRINCIPLES AND MORALS OF LIFE

Your principles are what you were given at birth, and as you grew up, you began to learn about what integrity is and what you want in life. You let it be known in your everyday life integrity is so important to always have because not only are you honest with yourself, but others who come across you can give you the same respect. In other words, respect yourself so others can respect you as well, and carry yourself with high standards in what you do, you don't have to be someone you are not, but be you. Be that person you were created to be, what you want in life and your happiness. Don't let anyone tell you how to live and who to live for you are your own boss. First, know your truth and embrace it every day, and don't forget to feed your self love everyday as you wake up every morning. Find a way to start a routine by putting yourself first before you start your day. I did even though it hasn't been easy because my health journey has also been a challenging journey but I continue to overcome it by taking care of myself and starting to go to the gym, best decision ever. This was the first moment that was going to also change my life in so many ways, it hasn't been easy because I would be lying. When your provider tells you that you are at risk and being overweight plays a big role. Yes, I told myself to sign up. I am at the gym and I am glad I did. I need that extra help with a personal trainer, and I am also glad I did that as well.

CHAPTER 49
CAN I LOVE AGAIN

Can I love again? I told myself, I cried after my divorce. I went through so many mixed emotions, not because I lost my husband. That was the best thing that could have happened for the best thing to come into my life. I questioned god. All my life, I felt like I was hit with many blows every time I was in a relationship. I blamed myself for what I was doing wrong. Was I the cause of this happening to me? I couldn't catch a break, and I told myself I didn't believe in love anymore and I would just stay alone for the rest of my life. I was tired, but as I am going through this healing journey that reminded me how I could love someone when I couldn't even love myself, my mind, body, and soul were craving that, so I had to take a step back and re-evaluate my choices I was making when it came to dating again, and now I am not afraid anymore to be by myself, because loving me was the best person I could have ever loved, and as I go through this journey it is preparing me for my King and future life partner that is just right around the corner. Sometimes, people go hunting for their future husband or wife or even go on online dating, and there is no need you wait patiently when you least expect that person will arrive at your doorstep. It's hard to fathom that, but this is so true. Being single again, yes, it's hard because, for one, you are healing from your previous relationship, but it's interesting how when you are going through your healing journey, you begin to meet new people unexpectedly to distract you from your pain but don't allow anyone to distract you because when you do you stop the healing process and put a bandaid on the wound that will just be re-open. There are many nats that are flying around waiting to find someone beautiful and valuable to catch and it goes for men to because they also have their fair share of heartache. People don't speak on it too much, but I hear of many good men treated really bad. I speak in general, fall in love with you first; don't rush love when it's your moment. It will happen. Just change your mindset about dating and just begin to heal and love yourself. Sometimes, for some, you can wait a moment, and some have to wait a lifetime to truly date again, but at the end of the day, no matter the time, no matter the journey, just enjoy the healing journey, and when that time happens, you will know. If you can't be alone or love yourself before another, then you truly don't know what love is. Loving yourself is a sign of peace and freedom. When you don't have that in a relationship, then it's not a relationship anymore. It's control. Be self-aware of your environment with family, partners, and friends, choose wisely, and if you have to cut people out of your life, then do it. You will be thankful you did. In order for new doors to open you sometimes have to close some that are just no longer meant for you. Well, here I am concluding this book of many more to come, but before I do, I want to close with this phrase I came up with. Pain, Power, and Purpose. The three P's. Your pain is your drive to push and not give up when you want to give up. Just know that tomorrow will be a better day. Power turns into your purpose. There can't be a purpose without a story and purpose without your power. You got this! Never give up, but remember to take one step at a time! I love you all. Remember to turn your pain into purpose. No matter the journey you're on, remember there's always a destination, don't worry how you will get there, just trust the process. This is just the beginning of my next chapter. Author, speaker, a college graduate with four degrees, and a single mom who has raised three beautiful children and continues her journey to help women reach their dreams and never give up on self! Always know that there is a light at the end of the tunnel. Remember, never stop loving yourself.

MY FINAL THOUGHTS

Remember, don't let anyone turn off your lights and keep on glowing in the path that you are walking in, and when your light gets dimmed, keep on pushing until you are glowing again, but remember, one step at a time, and turn that pain into purpose.

Gallery

Announcing my first book at home

Like mother like daughter, it is never too late for College

My Angel always watching over me Javier Campos

My first book event

She is always evolving

My Journey is just starting

My first published book, 2022

About Renee I Campos

Renee I Campos is an Author and speaker sharing her story and thrives on continuing to use writing to speak to women and share resilience and how writing has healed her in her journey after a traumatic fall-out relationship. She had to decide where her life was headed, whether it would be in a cold, isolated home with the fear of the man that she was married to or was going to stand up and break the silence. She is an Entrepreneur, author, and a survivor of domestic violence. Now, standing to fight and be that voice for women. Remember to love yourself and always put yourself first. You don't have to live in pain and sorrow. Turn your pain into purpose. Your nightmare is over. Renee's passion is to see women become women of Freedom, Independence, and Power. There is no excuse for abuse. Together, we can break the silence and be free!